Constructing
Social Problems

Social Problems and Social Issues

An Aldine de Gruyter Series of Texts and Monographs

SERIES EDITORS

John I. Kitsuse
University of California, Santa Cruz

Joseph W. Schneider
Drake University

Constructing Social Problems

Malcolm Spector

McGill University

John I. Kitsuse

University of California, Santa Cruz

ALDINE DE GRUYTER

New York

Aldine de Gruyter
A Division of Walter de Gruyter, Inc.
200 Saw Mill River Road
Hawthorne, New York 10532

Library of Congress Cataloging-in-Publication Data

Spector, Malcolm.
    Constructing social problems.

    Bibliography: p.
    Includes indexes.
    1. Social problems.   2. Social problems — Study and teaching.   I Kitsuse, John I.   II Title.
HN28.S7   1987   361.1   86-30214
ISBN 0-202-30337-3 (pbk.)

Printed in the United States of America

10   9   8   7   6   5   4   3   2

Contents

v

Acknowledgments

This work began in a graduate seminar at Northwestern University. We gratefully acknowledge the interest and assistance of the participants in that seminar who helped us set this project in motion. Several earlier papers, published in *Social Problems* and *Teaching Sociology,* benefitted from the criticisms of Sheldon Messinger, Howard Becker, Allan Schnaiberg, John Walton, Joseph Gusfield, and Kai Erikson. Sally Mae Spector aided greatly in the final editing, untangling many an awkward sentence. We also wish to acknowledge the exceptional editorial intelligence of James F. Short, Jr. His counsel was invaluable and always pressed us to clarify the logic of our statements. As we have not always followed the advice of our colleagues, we relieve them of responsibility for whatever defects of omission and commission that remain. Finally, our thanks to Mrs. Alice Lamming for typing the manuscript.

1

Introduction

There is no adequate definition of social problems within sociology, and there is not and never has been a sociology of social problems. That observation is the point of departure of this book. It is our aim to provide such a definition and to prepare the ground for the empirical study of social problems. We are cognizant that our opening statement will seem extreme, perhaps shocking, to sociologists who have, over a period of fifty years, written treatises on social problems, produced textbooks cataloging the nature, distribution, and causes of those problems, and devoted many years to teaching courses listed as social problems. Indeed, how is our statement to be justified in view of the large literature which has established a "sociology of" a wide range of social problems—the sociology of race relations, prostitution, poverty, crime, mental illness, and so forth?

The term "social problem" has itself been more a rubric for presenting sociological wisdom to undergraduates than the focus of theory and research of a specified subject matter. It may be helpful to illustrate this view with two definitions from current texts that illustrate the way "social problem" is treated as a technical term. Our first example not only strains the limits of grammar, but contains terms so abstract that we have no idea how they might be specified empirically. Birenbaum and Sagarin offer the following definition:

> *A social problem exists when the collective society is rent by, at the very least, a public recognition that there is a sector of society, represented by its practices, which threatens or prevents others or themselves from establishing or maintaining their claims to membership. (1972:16)*

Raab and Selznick present a second example. Their definition reflects the good will of the concerned citizen, but lacks the precision and clarity that are essential to any technical definition.

> *A social problem exists when organized society's ability to order relationships among people seems to be failing; when its institutions are*

1

faltering, its laws are being flouted, the transmission of its values from one generation to the next is breaking down, the framework of social expectations is being shaken. (1959:6)

What constitutes "collective society," or a "public recognition"; which "practices," and how do they constitute "threats"; which "relationships," and how do we know when they "fail"; when are institutions "faltering," laws being "flouted," and so on? We shall not belabor the point that these examples of definitions of social problems are imprecise and ambiguous. Suffice it to say, it is evident that the usual care and craft that sociologists exercise in their research and theoretical writings have not been applied to their work on social problems.

Let us consider the example of crime. Sociologists have posed a variety of questions about crime. They have produced typologies of different kinds of crimes and criminals, examined rates of crime over time and in different geographical areas, and have analyzed the characteristics that differentiate criminals from noncriminals in their search for explanations of crime. They have evaluated efforts to prevent crime as well as to rehabilitate criminals. More recently they have examined the interactions between criminals, their victims, and the police, and they have published ethnographic studies of various criminal occupations. These are all aspects of the sociology of crime.

None of these studies, however, require the definition of crime as a social problem, and none specifically use this concept in their analysis of crime. To put it another way, what is added to our understanding of crime by pointing out that it is a social problem? Nothing is added unless invoking the concept is based on an explicit consideration of the question, "Is crime a social problem, and if so, what constitutes the social problem of crime?"

Although an answer to the first part of the question might seem to be an emphatic yes, what is the answer to the second part? What is it that makes crime a social problem? Is it the absolute number of crimes? Is it the types of crime committed? Is it the increase in the rate of some crimes or of crime in general? Does crime become a social problem when "the streets are no longer safe at night"? Is crime considered a problem because the police are inefficient in solving crime? Is the issue police corruption as manifested in payoffs, bribes, shakedowns, protection rackets, and violence, or in the collusion between the police and organized criminals? Is it that the crimes of the powerful and prominent are ignored, that social class or racial inequities exist in the criminal justice system? Is it that victims of rape are callously treated, and racial, ethnic, or age groups are harassed and brutalized? Is the social problem of crime indicated by the leniency of the courts in sentencing convicted felons? Or, is it that the rights of the accused to the due process of law are abridged by the criminal justice system? Is crime to be considered a social problem on any or all of these grounds? If these questions had been as thoroughly researched as the "sociology of crime" discussed above, we might be able to discuss, not crime, but the social problem of crime.

One sociologist has argued that one type of crime—organized crime—is *not* a social problem. A close examination of his argument will clarify the distinction we wish to make between the study of crime and the study of the social problem of crime. Donald R. Cressey worked as a consultant to the National Crime Commission, especially on the Task Force on Organized Crime. He became convinced that the organized criminal activities of the Mafia are more costly to the American public than all other kinds of crime combined. Yet he also noted that there was very little public awareness of these costs and dangers, and little demand that "something be done about" the Mafia. In short, Cressey argues that organized crime is not a social problem and offers the following analysis:

> *First, information on organized crime has, by and large, been presented to the public in a sensational manner. Police, well aware of the sensationalism present in televised Congressional hearings involving unsavory characters; in newspaper accounts of the activities of "muscle men," "gorillas," and "meat hooks"; and in popular books about "The Mafia Menace," say that the public is misled because the mass media insist on playing "cops and robbers" and "gang buster." Newspapermen find it virtually impossible to depict the participants as anything but gangsters who prey principally on each other. For example, there are a few newspaper accounts in which Mr. Lucchese is called "Mr. Lucchese" or Mr. Ricca is called "Mr. Ricca. . . ." "Mr. Lucchese," when he was alive, could possibly have been someone who was corrupting my labor union, but "Three Finger Brown" could only have been a somewhat fictitious character in a "cops and robbers" story. Similarly, usury is almost always called "the juice racket," and this terminology lets the reader believe that the activity has nothing to do with him or the safety of his community. . . . Most of us can understand the seriousness of usury, bankruptcy fraud, and bribery, but we have a hard time realizing that our friends and neighbors are, in the long run, the victims of "the juice racket," "the scam racket," or "the fix." Probably of even more relevance to any prevailing skepticism is the fact that the murder of a La Cosa Nostra member by men acting under orders from the victim's "family Boss" is invariably described by the mass media as a "hit" or a "gangland slaying." In fact, a high proportion of such murders are executions of members who have secretly left the criminals' camp to join the forces of law, order, and decency. Calling the murder a "hit" makes it all but impossible for the reader to realize that control of a community's economic and political affairs by an alliance of criminals is serious business, certainly as serious as would be control of these affairs by Communists. (1967:104-5)*

Cressey then argues that organized crime is not defined as a social problem and that it probably will not soon be so defined. He presents three reasons why individuals, the general public, or civic groups do not demand reform or elimination of organized crime, do not aid the police in such work, and do not perceive the liabilities and dangers posed by La Cosa Nostra:

> *First, the American confederation of criminals thrives because a large minority of citizens demand the illicit goods and services that it has for sale. . . . Organized crime cannot become a social problem until a much broader segment of society perceives that the cost of the services provided is too high. (1967:107)*

> *Second, a large proportion of the persons demanding illicit goods and services believe that they are being supplied by criminals who are unorganized and who, for that matter, are not very criminal. A nice old man who accepts a few bets from the patrons of his restaurant does not seem very dangerous. . . . "Gambling" cannot become a social problem until it is widely known that bookmakers are not gamblers . . . "organization," not gambling, is the phenomenon to worry about. (1967:108)*

> *Third, "organized crime" is not against the law. What is against the law is smuggling and selling narcotics, bookmaking, usury, murder, extortion, conspiracy, and the like. . . . For this reason, data cannot be routinely compiled on organized crime in the way that they are routinely compiled on, say, burglary and automobile theft. But the issue involves more than questions of assembling data. The legal lacunae permit directors of illicit businesses to remain immune from arrest, prosecution, and imprisonment unless they themselves violate specific criminal laws such as those prohibiting individuals from selling narcotics . . . it makes it difficult for a wide segment of society to perceive "organized crime" as a social problem. (1967:108-9)*

Cressey's analysis is more than a description of the absence of widespread definitions of organized crime as a social problem. He clearly believes that "objectively" organized crime exists, and his analysis is in part a complaint that it is not "subjectively" recognized and treated as if it existed. He clearly separates the existence of organized crime as a social problem, which he maintains does *not* exist, from a highly organized confederation of criminals who engage in a wide range of criminal activities, which he is convinced *does* exist. Cressey closes his discussion with the following observation:

> *In the "social problems" area of sociology especially, it is only a slight exaggeration to say that "a social problem was created because certain data were assembled," rather than "data on a social problem were assembled." From this perspective, one important goal of the Commis-*

sions's Task Force on Organized Crime was the creation of a social problem . . . we joined the ranks of men who are paid to recognize organized crime as a social problem. These men, mostly police officers and prosecutors . . . when they plead for "education of the public," they are asking that a major social problem be created. (1967:106)

We have presented Cressey's analysis at some length to provide a detailed example of the distinction between what we shall call *the objective conditions* and the definitions of them as social problems. This distinction is central to our reformulation of the sociology of social problems. We shall argue that while the former has long provided the basis for the study of a wide range of social phenomena, the latter logically provides the subject matter for a sociology of social problems—subject matter that has been almost entirely ignored and unexplored.

We shall examine the failure of the social problems literature to explore the question of how social problems are defined, and then attempt to begin such an analysis. It is, of course, not true that concern with the *subjective side* of social problems is completely absent in this literature. Even the traditional and dominant functionalist approach occasionally acknowledges that the existence of objective conditions does not in itself constitute social problems. For example, Robert Nisbet, in the introduction to a leading social problems text, underlines the importance of subjective criteria and the relevance of moral enterprise in the definition of social problems:

A social problem cannot be said to exist until it is defined as one. The way of behavior involved may be fixed and may be found among many peoples. But unless the way of behavior is defined as a violation of some norm, unless it is regarded by large numbers of people as being repugnant to moral consciousness, it cannot be termed a social problem. . . . We are obliged, as sociologists, to recognize that social problems are inseparably joined to subjective awareness of a particular set of norms. . . . There is a reciprocal relation between moral consciousness in a society and the perceived existence of social problems. . . . No social problem exists for any people unless it has been defined as a social problem. The subjective element is inescapable. (1971:2-3)

In the same Merton and Nisbet text, Cohen and Short refer, in more restrained language, to the distinction between the study of crime and the social problem of crime:

To some extent the study of the social problems relating to crime is separable from the study of crime itself. Social problems may be differently defined by different segments of a population. To some, the need to suppress certain kinds of criminality is the problem; to others, the crimi-

nality is a minor issue, and the conduct of the police or the puritanical zeal of the legislature is the problem. A social problem can become a major social issue and then subside, without the situation it concerns having undergone any significant change. (1971:98-9)

These statements, however, have not led their authors to explore, describe, and analyze these definitional processes. They are embedded in analyses of the objective conditions of crime and other phenomena, simply presented as prefatory statements that have little consequence for guiding the selection of subject matter, the data, or the analyses they make. In Chapter 2 we shall examine in detail the leading contemporary expression of the traditional functionalist formulation of social problems.

Some writers have attempted to focus on the definitional process of social problems. This group has always represented a minority position within this area of specialization, and more generally, within the discipline of sociology. They have expressed their views primarily through articles that criticize the dominant "objective" approach for its failure to deal systematically with the definitional processes. In reviewing this critical literature—some of which extends back into the 1920's—we have found that while writers interested in the process of definition have soundly rejected the dominant "objective" tradition, they have largely failed to initiate an alternative line of investigation. We have also been struck by the paradox in which writers who bared the inadequacies of the dominant view of social problems and deviance fell into the very theoretical impasse that they criticized with such penetrating logic.

The writers who contributed to this critical literature present us with a puzzle: why and how did they, armed with a radical vision of the sociology of social problems, and with a vigorous critique and reasoned rejection of the traditional approach, fail to initiate their own tradition of research and theory? Further, how is it that they all drifted back toward the concerns that they had criticized and rejected? In Chapter 3 we describe these efforts to conceptualize the definitional process as the subject matter of a sociology of social problems. The classic statements of Case, Frank, Waller, and Fuller and Myers, and the more recent restatements by Blumer, Becker, Mauss, and others provide the core insight that we hope to develop in the remainder of this book. It is our view that the definitional approach has always been presented in conceptually ambiguous or intentionally eclectic formulations. No one has ever attempted to pursue the implications of this position singlemindedly to their logical conclusion.

In Chapter 4, we ask why definitional processes should have escaped the systematic attention of social problems theorists—even those who intentionally set out to make them the focus of their investigations. We shall compare the development of the *definitional approach in social problems* with that of the so-called *labeling school of deviance* to show how the two theoretical perspectives have encountered similar problems. We view these problems to be a consequence of a failure, common in the development of both approaches, to consider the sociologist as an active participant in the process of definition, and we will outline a sociology of knowledge perspective on this theoretical issue.

In Chapter 5 we present our own definition of social problems, relying heavily on the notion of claims-making and responding activities. Our goal is to construct a definition amenable to empirical elaboration in which the process of definition and not the "objective conditions" is the central concern. Chapter 6 provides an empirical case in point, the kind of research we think logically follows from our definition. By presenting the data of such research in a raw, descriptive form, we hope to make clear that our definition does not simply lead to another analysis of the traditional social problems material nor to another explanation of those "objective conditions" that have conventionally occupied sociologists of social problems. The concept of *natural history* in the study of social problems is reviewed and rehabilitated in Chapter 7, and we propose a hypothetical model to guide subsequent social problems research. In Chapter 8 we report on our efforts to use the formulation developed in this book to organize assignments and projects for an undergraduate course in social problems.

SOCIAL PROBLEMS: SOME EXAMPLES

In the remainder of this chapter we give examples of the kinds of materials we think should become the subject of the sociology of social problems. We present these materials as part of the introduction for a specific purpose; we want to specify for the reader the kinds of materials we think the traditional functional view of social problems has chosen to ignore or to assume as nonproblematic. And when we argue that the definitional approach was unfaithful to its radical vision, these materials will provide examples of what we consider to be the logical implications of that view. Thus, when we say that the proponents of this approach were deflected from the logic of their analysis, we want the reader to know where we think that logic leads in theory and research. Finally, when we say that we are trying to lay the foundation for a study of definitional processes, we want to have ready examples of such definitions.

We have chosen our examples to suggest or illustrate various strategies for studying the processes through which definitions of social problems are constructed, sustained, changed, or abandoned. Examples are intentionally concrete and descriptive. We wish to avoid the common practice of sociologists of referring to how "society" defines this or that, e.g., "If society would stop defining homosexuality as a disease, more people would come out of the closets." This leaves unspecified how "society" might define something; nor does it suggest where one might look for "society's" definitions. Phrases such as "the culture defines what is good and what is bad," or "a society's values determine what is defined as deviant'' are similarly unhelpful as guides for empirical inquiry. This type of reference to definitions certainly reinforces the conclusion that such processess may not easily be studied.

Definitions are produced by those who argue for and act on their conceptions of social conditions. Rather than speaking of "society" in the abstract, we prefer to locate those specific organizations, groups, or individuals who take positions and propose specific definitions. Thus, while it does not make sense to say that "society" defines homosexuality, it is sensible to state that the American Psychiatric Association has such a definition—as did the Wolfenden Commission in England—as well as numerous legislative and gay liberation groups. Let us examine some concrete instances where definitions have been constructed.

DEFINITIONS OF WORDS

One way to begin a study of definitions is to examine the specific vocabularies that are used to describe and classify a condition. Definitions of social problems are expressed in terms that describe the condition, reflect attitudes toward the condition, and give numerous other hints as to how that condition is considered offensive or problematic. Groups often vie for control of the definition of a problem. When one group wins, its vocabulary may be adopted and institutionalized while the concepts of the opposing groups fall into obscurity. When terminologies change, when new terms are invented, or existing terms are given new meanings, these actions signal that something important has happened to the career or history of a social problem.

The history of the definition and the classification of persons who are today considered mentally retarded in varying degree provide a good example of how invented words identify and shape popular conceptions of social conditions and the development of social problems. A large number of terms exist in the English language to refer to this population. Two of these, *idiot* and *imbecile,* have a long history in the English language; others like *educable, mentally handicapped* (EMH) are technical, bureaucratic categories of recent vintage. One term, however, *moron,* will not be found in any dictionary prior to the twentieth century, although it has ancient etymological roots. The word comes from the Greek root *moros,* meaning foolish, as for example, in the word *sophomore,* a wise fool.

The word moron was invented by the Committee on Classification of the American Association of Medical Directors of Institutions for the Feeble-minded. It first appeared in print in the report of that committee in the *Journal of Psycho-Asthenics* (1910, v. XV, no. 2, p. 61). The invention of this term was part of the final shift from a pathological to a psychological conception of feeblemindedness. The former used terms such as hydrocephalic, micro-cephalic, mongoloid, and cretin, which referred to physical pathologies that are associated with feeblemindedness.

While it had long been recognized by practitioners that each of these classifications contained persons of widely differing degrees of impairment, it was not until the development of the intelligence test by Binet that this came to seem anomalous. Intelligence testing originated in France for use in screening children in the Parisian school system. Its purpose was to identify children who "could not benefit" from instruction, and who would disrupt the class-room. Reports of these procedures began to appear in American journals just after the turn of the century. Medical directors of institutions for the feeble-minded were particularly interested in them, and several, including Henry H. Goddard, began translating and administering the tests to institutionalized populations. The prospect of developing an exact quantitative index of impair-ment, independent of physical anomalies or pathologies, led to a search for a new basis of classification.

The intelligence test allowed an exact quantitative comparison of per-formances independent of other diagnostic and clinical symptoms. The prospect of its use led to a variety of proposals for taxonomic schemes. Some were based simply on mental age, others proposed three or four broad categories. Still others sought to combine three categories with a threefold subdivision of each category, arriving at a "decimal" classification. The following scheme was finally adopted by the committee.

Feebleminded Children

New definitions	Classification/score		Binet mental age
Morons	High grade	(9)	
	Middle grade	(8)	8–12
	Low grade	(7)	
Imbeciles	High grade	(6)	
	Middle grade	(5)	3–7
	Low grade	(4)	
Idiots	High grade	(3)	
	Middle grade	(2)	0–2
	Low grade	(1)	

The new classification was specifically based on the Binet tests, which classify the mental age of children. It has three broad categories, each one subdivided into three grades. The number following each grade is its decimal category, with the normal child obtaining a score of 10. No mention is made of children of superior intelligence, or of variations among normally intelligent children, nor is there any mention of adults. Goddard saw the following advantage to this decimal scheme:

> This [decimal classification] might be of some use incidentally, in that it would be fairly intelligent if we were to say to a stranger, this child classifies five on a scale of ten. Of course, such an explanation would be incomplete because they would not know where the beginning was or hardly the end of the series. Still, it would mean much more than it now means to say to such a person, we call this child an idio-imbecile. (Goddard, quoted in Rogers, 1910a:65)

Thus were the terms *idiot* and *imbecile*, which had a common usage in the English language, redefined as technical terms with precise quantitative meanings. Dictionaries soon referred to idiots as persons with a mental age of zero to two and imbeciles as persons with a mental age of three to seven. *Moron* however, was an entirely new term, indicating a problem of definition that had little precedent in the previous pathological classification, that is, the borderline case. When gross physical abnormalities were the basis for definitions of feeblemindedness, the borderline case was not a terribly controversial issue. Development of a continuum of intelligence, with quantitative scores distinguishing fine differences, thrust into prominence the problem of drawing a line between the normal and subnormal.

The committee found that two existing terms could be used for those with profound and moderate degrees of impairment, but no suitable term could be found for those falling just below the borderline between normal and retarded. The group considered the term *feebleminded*, but rejected it on the grounds that it was commonly used to refer to all those with mental impairment. Other three-category classification schemes proposed were idiot, idio-imbecile, and imbecile, and psycho-asthenia, amentia, and mental debility. The members wanted a simple word to designate the borderline case that would be understandable to the public and capable of being readily incorporated into English usage. Further, they wanted a term whose root could be easily used as a combining form, which could be transformed into an adjective, and which could refer both to a person and to the condition itself. With these considerations in mind, the head of the Greek Department of the Minnesota State University, Professor John C. Hutchinson, was consulted. He proposed two alternatives—one based on the root *proximate* (conveying the idea of just next to normal) and the other based on the root *moros*. The committee chose moron, with the parallel constructions of *moronic* as the adjective and *moronity* as the state of being a moron.

The new classification was launched in the *Journal of Psycho-Asthenics,* both with the published report of the committee on classification and in an editorial. Subsequent issues of the journal show that most writers adopted the new terminology, perhaps enforced by editorial policy. (A book reviewer several years later chastised an author for not using the new terms.) Psychologists who were quick to develop the field of mental testing adopted the terminology of the committee, and dictionaries included both the new term moron and the technical redefinitions of idiot and imbecile.

One aim of the committee, however, was not realized. Henry Goddard, arguing in favor of the new word moron, claimed:

> *It has the advantage also of not being already in use in English in any sense. Consequently, we would have no quarrel or necessity for saying that we use it in a special way. We would simply define its meaning once [and] for all, and by using it, make it stand for what we want. (Rogers, 1910a:65)*

Implicit in this statement was the concern that once the term had achieved acceptance, a small group of professionals might not be able to control the ways in which others would use the term. The committee probably anticipated that moron would acquire pejorative connotations similar to idiot and imbecile. Even the term *backward children*, which they fashioned to refer to those who scored just above morons, was a euphemism. The editorial announcing the new classification clearly expressed the concern that "charlatans" and inexperienced people might abuse the Binet mental tests and the system of classification.

> *To secure reliable data concerning feebleminded children, one must know from experience something of the nature of the class he is working with, and must possess that peculiar, and not altogether common faculty of securing the absolute confidence of the child, and hence, the ability to obtain a full response in each case. . . .*
>
> *The question of diagnosis of mental defect is often involved in court practice and it can readily be seen how easily unprincipled charlatans might exploit alleged laboratory tests in the interest of criminal offenses against feebleminded women in the higher grades. (Rogers, 1910 b:71)*

The committee, of course, could not prevent this from happening. The first mention of moron in the *New York Times Index* refers to a court case where a lawyer pleaded that his client was a moron. The questions he had been asked to test his mental age at Bellevue Hospital concerned the difference between a horse and a cow, and between a bird and a butterfly *(New York*

Times, May 26, 1922, 15:2). The judge in the case, commenting on the testimony of the presumed moron, said; "This witness seems to be as well equipped as some college graduates."

The next day, the *New York Times* carried an editorial under the head "Testing the Mental Test." It remarked on the court case, the judge's remarks and the increased use of tests in every corner of society (as in job placements) and then commented as follows:

> *A moron has been not inaptly defined as a man, who thought he might not be able to get into college, if he once did so, couldn't help [but] graduate. (New York Times, May 27, 1922, 12:4)*

The career of this term was not limited to expedient adaptations, opportunistic misuse, populare and simple-minded distortions, or pejorative connotations. Clifford Shaw, in his *Natural History of a Delinquent Career,* provides us with a view of the word *moron* in 1928. This volume describes the life of Sidney Blotzman, a young criminal who, among other things, was convicted of rape and sentenced to twenty years in prison. Chapter I is entitled "Labeled a Moron," and contains the following account of the use of that term:

> *The attitudes [toward all offenders guilty of sex assaults upon women] which are essentially emotional in character, find their expression in various opprobrious epithets, among which the term "moron" is perhaps the most common. This term, which is technically used to define a person with an intelligence quotient of 50-70, denoting mental, rather than moral deficiency, has become in popular usage synonymous with rapist .... Popularly, the term implied that the person is degenerate, devoid of moral sensibilities and perhaps not capable of conforming to the traditional standards of conventional society .... The use of the term "moron" for rapist by newspapers and the public goes back historically to the period when early studies seemed to indicate a high correlation between feeble-mindedness and delinquency. Recent studies have largely discredited this early assumption. . . . In keeping with this popular attitude Sidney was labeled as a "moron" dispite the fact that he possessed very superior intelligence, having an intelligence quotient of 119. (1931:4)*

We have presented an example in which the documentation of the invention of a new term is particularly complete. It is not intended as a full treatment of the impact of intelligence testing on conceptions of mental retardation. We wish, rather, to suggest how a focus on the definition of conditions (in this case degrees of mental retardation) leads to examination of materials generally ignored by students of social problems. This conception of social problems directs us to investigate the activities of specific and identifiable individuals (not "society") who are engaged in defining conditions in particular terms with specific (recorded) purposes in mind.

THE LIBRARY OF CONGRESS TREATMENT OF HOMOSEXUALITY

In a letter to the editor of *Library Journal* (January 10, 1972) Stephen Wolf, a librarian at the University of Massachusetts, complained that the Library of Congress (commonly referred to as LC) was "unquestioningly perpetrating ancient antigay prejudices and superstitions." Wolf, a member of an ad hoc group within the American Library Association, the Social Responsibilities Round Table Task Force on Gay Liberation, charged that two books dealing with the gay liberation movement had been assigned numbers reserved for books on abnormal sexual relations, sexual crimes, and sexual perversions. Wolf pointed out:

> *The very point of the gay liberation movement is that gays are not "abnormal" or "perverse," yet LC cataloging still persists in repeating this vulgar error.*

Wolf was referring to a system of classification that the LC uses to sort and catalog the millions of books and other items received each year. These categories are in turn used by virtually all libraries in North America and by all library users searching for a particular book or books on a given subject. The categories and definitions of this system of classification determine the organization of the card catalog, the call number assigned to each book, and the way books are arranged on the shelves. Thus, it is a highly centralized policy-making instrument. When the LC changes the way it classifies a subject, virtually all North American libraries follow suit.

Wolf made a specific complaint that books on gay liberation were assigned the number HQ 76. His objection may be graphically displayed in the following chart that section of LC classification that included homosexuality. The indentations, like any outlining system, denote material that is subsumed under the larger category, while categories that align with each other are not so included.

Social Groups: The Family, Marriage, Woman
　　Sex Relations HQ 12-471
　　　Abnormal Sex Relations (including sexual crimes) HQ 71-471
　　　Sexual Perversion in Woman HQ 73
　　　Homosexuality HQ 76
　　　Sadism, Masochism, Fetishism, etc. HQ 79
　　　Prostitution HQ 101-449
(From Library of Congress, 1950, with supplementary pages, reprinted 1965)

In a letter dated February 10, 1972, the assistant director of cataloging of the LC wrote Mr. Wolf that the classification of homosexuality had been changed. He agreed that works on gay liberation were misclassified as works on abnormal sex relations. Therefore a new category on Gay Liberation Movements was created. Furthermore, the section on abnormal sexual relations was revised. In place of the old scheme the following one was instituted:

Social Groups: The Family, Marriage, Woman

  Sexual Life HQ 12-471

   Sexual Deviations, including sex crimes HQ 71-72

   Homosexuality, Lesbianism HQ 76

    Gay Liberation Movement. Homophile Movement HQ 76.5

   Transvestism HQ 77

   Sadism, Masochism, Fetishism, etc. HQ 79

   Prostitution HQ 101-449

(From Library of Congress, 1974)

The alignment of categories indicates a far different conception of sexual life than the system used in 1965. Homosexuality is no longer a subcategory of abnormal relations; the neutral term *Lesbianism* has replaced "Sexual Perversion in Woman." Prostitution is no longer classified as an abnormal sexual relation, but only as one variety of sexual life. The change also removes sadism, masochism, and fetishism as entries under *Abnormal Sex Relations,* and transvestism now has a number of its own in contrast to its former place, presumably under *etc.*

In a press release, Wolf described the activities of the task force which claimed credit as the instrument of the change in classification:

> *Under the leadership of Barbara Gittings, the "homophile bibliophiles" of the Task Force on Gay Liberation are working to bring about still further changes by seeing that books and other materials emphasizing the healthy, positive aspects of gay life are made both readily available to libraries and easily accessible to individual readers. To implement this goal the Task Force compiles a frequently updated "basic collection" bibliography of books, periodicals, pamphlets, and articles. . . . For all too long the only "literature" about gay life-style was the pseudo-scientific sickness-theory tracts of Drs. Bieber, Bergler, Reuben, etc. Today, as the Task Force works to make more and beter gay-affirmative literature available to gays and straights, society's antigay prejudices and stereotypes are beginning to disappear. The Library of Congress revisions are a clear signpost of that change.*

Before moving on to a third example of social problems definitional processes, we will briefly compare some features of the two cases. In both, a change in definitions was traced to the activities of specific groups of individuals. These individuals were engaged in technical activities within the confines of their professions, creating new distinctions in their definitions and redefinitions of social phenomena. Their activities may be thought to be a part of "society's" responses to mental retardation and various forms of sexual relations. The categories and meanings that they have created have direct consequences for the ways such phenomena are conceived, evaluated, and treated.

The committee on classification provided authoritative standards for school officials as they incorporated the Binet tests in their educational programs, as well as for the parents who sought help and guidance in their efforts to monitor the educational performance of their children. Similarly, the decision of the LC meant that hundreds of libraries added subject cards on gay liberation movements in their catalogs. While the reclassification sponsored by the LC may not correspond to the categories of thought of many people, they are the categories that members must use in seeking information or literature. These subject headings and the cross references linking them constitute the system by which knowledge about any topic recognized by the LC is made available. Not only did the LC policy remove references to sexual perversion, the new classification had the effect of grouping together under one call number items on gay liberation previously scattered among psychiatric treatment of homosexuality and discussions of sexual crime and perversion. In short, both decisions formally classified ways of thinking about social phenomena.

As status distinctions become the focus of attention of reformers and crusaders, the labels and technical classifications of agencies and professional organizations have become more visible as objects of controversy. The classification of homosexuality is simply a case in point. Other social movements within the American Library Association are demanding that the LC cease using the term *Negro,* replacing it with *Afro-American* and *Black.* Still others are demanding that such categories as *Women as Artist* be changed to *Women Artist.* (For a discussion of sexism in library classification, see Foskett, 1971. For an exchange on the treatment of the American Indian in the LC subject heads, see Yen-Ran Yeh, 1971, and Frosio, 1971.) There are also demands for the elimination of subject heads like *Jews as Businessmen* and *Yellow Peril* (Berman, 1971). Much of the work of catalogers does not bear on social problems activities, but they routinely deal with subjects that become the focus of controversies. Thus, while organizationally the decision to change all references to *Electronic Calculators* to *Computers* involved massive clerical work, the impetus for the change does not appear to have been generated by morally indignant groups, nor does it appear that the change has offended the moral sensibilities of any segment of the population. However, it is possible that any category or set of definitions may become the focus of such concern.

THE YELLOW PAGES

Many other classification systems exist that might provide the subject matter for an analysis of how definitions of social phenomena change. We shall discuss some, such as the *Readers' Guide to Periodical Literature,* the *Public Affairs Information Service,* or the *Index Medicus,* in the final chapter on teaching social problems. The yellow pages or classified telephone directory is also a system of subject categories that participate in the definitions of social problems. The emergence of a new category, such as *Pollution Control Industry,* may indicate and facilitate the activities of a group of companies that want to promote certain kinds of services or exploit certain demands or desires of the population. Similarly, the fact that one cannot find *Abortionist* or *Abortion Clinic* under those headings suggests that its newly acquired legal status has not yet disseminated into every aspect of the society.

Those who create categories for the yellow pages make definitions available to advertisers and consumers as librarians do when they change classifications, or professional associations do when they invent technical terms. The following example, although somewhat humorous, and not closely tied to traditionally conceived social problems subject matter, provides insight into creating new categories for the yellow pages.

> *I was thinking about what to do for a second career when a call came in from a lady who wanted me to advertise my first career in the Yellow Pages: she suggested that my company take a boldface listing under Advertising Agencies. . . . She was very nice—the kind of person you can trust—so I decided to confide in her on my second career and to see if that could be listed, too. She thought it was a wonderful idea and asked what heading I wanted to list. I told her "under Philosophers" and there was a long pause. "Are you a philosopher?" she asked.*

> *"Yes, I am." I said. "I'm not a very good one, but I notice you list a dentist in there who isn't very good and at least one plumber who is downright incompetent."*

> *When she still seemed uncertain, I tried to win her confidence with the hint that I might consider boldface type, but that didn't seem to do the trick. She asked me to hold the line, and I was left to doodle, jotting down notes for my first ad under the heading of Philosophers. I thought I might use the name Aristotle, which has a certain something that my own name lacks.*

ARISTOTLE
A trusted name in philosophy
for over 2000 years.

Rates reasonable.

The lady came back on the line and said that they didn't have a category for philosophers. Would they start one for Aristotle? Well, that would depend. If the heading is in use in at least three other cities, then her agency would put through a routine request to the telephone company to start it in this city.

"But I checked the Philadelphia directory," she warned. "They don't have any philosophers, either."

Aristotle needed help from Socrates. "Do you mean that if there aren't any philosophers now, there can never be any philosophers?"

No, that wasn't right. She said the telephone company understands that new products and services have to get their start somewhere. If the heading isn't in use in three other cities, her agency can put in a special request to the phone company for a new heading. If they feel there would be sufficient public demand for philosophers, then they might approve the request. Short of that, they might consent to a cross-reference listing (but not in the boldface) in the index.

That way, if you were looking for a philosopher, your fingers would walk through Packing Materials—Excelsior, Pails, Pallets and Skids, Pamphlet Preparation, Paraffin, Pastors, Pastries, Pattern Perforators, Peanut Oil, Pet Insurance, Pews, and Philatelists; then you would come to the entry:

Philosophers—See
ADVERTISING AGENCIES

I've since learned that to use the name Aristotle, I'll have to pay eleven dollars to register it under the Fictitious Names Act, even if that was his real name. You pay the eleven dollars, because they say so.

(Van Dine, 1972, 6-7)

PSYCHIATRIC NOMENCLATURE ON HOMOSEXUALITY

A final example shows how a system of classification may provide the focal point of a previously ill-defined controversy. Gay liberation organizations have often expressed their opposition to the view of the psychiatric establishment that homosexuals could or should be given psychiatric treatment. Beginning in the late 1960's gay groups expressed their opposition to this view by disrupting panels at psychiatric conventions. This technique, which they called "zapping," gained considerable publicity, but led to no apparent change in psychiatric attitudes or policy toward homosexuality. At one such convention the Gay Activist Alliance (GAA) of New York was zapping a panel on the use of behavior modification techniques (such as electric shocks) to modify sexual preferences. Ron Gold, the publicity director of the GAA, met and had a heated discussion with Robert Spitzer, a psychiatrist and member of the American Psychiatric Association Committee on Nomenclature.

This committee publishes a pamphlet called the *Diagnostic and Statistical Manual* (DSM). It is a list of psychiatric disorders, a classification or nosology of all the things that could possible "go wrong" with a person in the psychiatric realm. This manual is not a prominent public document. It is used primarily to keep hospital records and to serve as a standard reference for communications between the psychiatrist and insurance companies and other bureaucratic organizations.

The first edition of the DSM, published in 1952, made no direct reference to homosexuality. The second edition, however, published in 1966, through a policy of subdividing categories and making finer distinctions, lists homosexuality as one of the subdivisions of sexual disorders. See below.

Diagnostic and Statistical Manual—I

52   Sociopathic Personality Disturbance

52.0	*Antisocial reaction*
52.1	*Dyssocial reaction*
52.2	*Sexual deviation*
52.3	*Alcoholic (addiction)*
52.4	*Drug addiction*

From: American Psychiatric Association, 1952:85.

Diagnostic and Statistical Manual—II

302   Sexual Deviations

.0	*Homosexuality*
.1	*Fetishism*
.2	*Pedophilia*
.3	*Transvestism*
.4	*Exhibitionism*
.5	*Voyeurism*

.6 *Sadism*

.7 *Masochism*

.8 *Other sexual deviation*

.9 *Unspecified sexual deviation*

From: American Psychiatric Association, 1968:10.

In the first edition there are no subdivisions of sexual behavior. Homosexuality is not specifically itemized, nor given its own number, although it is referred to in passing in the three-sentence explanation (page 39) of the entire category. In the second edition homosexuality is prominently displayed with its own number.

Gold asked Spitzer if he would arrange a meeting between the committee on nomenclature and gay groups in order to discuss the issue of the categories for homosexuality. Spitzer did arrange such a meeting and it took place in New York in February 1973. At this meeting a number of gay groups combined to present evidence that homosexuality could not be viewed as a psychiatric disorder, refuting the traditional psychiatric authorities. Spitzer took it upon himself to respond for the committee to the presentation. He drafted a resolution and organized a panel discussion on homosexuality for the meeting of the American Psychiatric Association in May.

The panel, composed of five psychiatrists and Ronald Gold as the representative of the GAA, was held in Honolulu. Irving Bieber and Charles Socarides, particular targets of the GAA for their adherence to the "sickness" view of homosexuality, argued for the retention of the existing classification. The other psychiatrists on the panel expressed varying views in favor of changing the classifications. The panel was extremely well attended and this encouraged Spitzer to ask the committee on nomenclature to delete the category "homosexuality" and substitute instead, "sexual orientation disturbance." (See Spitzer, 1973, for an account of this meeting.)

The committee on nomenclature sent the proposal to the council on research and development, which approved it unanimously and sent it to the board of trustees for final approval. The approval came in December 1973 and was announced at a press confeence at APA headquarters in Washington, D.C. The new category was proclaimed and accompanied with a statement that homosexuality should not in itself be considered a mental illness:

The category of homosexuality is now replaced by "sexual orientation disturbance" which is described as follows: "This category is for individuals whose sexual interests are directed primarily toward people of the same sex who are either disturbed by, in conflict with, or wish to change their sexual orientation. This diagnostic category is distinguished from homosexuality, which by itself does not necessarily constitute a psychiatric disorder. Homosexuality per se is one form of sexual behavior, and like other forms of sexual behavior which are not by themselves psychiatric disorders, is not listed in this nomenclature of mental disorders. (American Psychiatric Association, press release, December 15, 1972.)

Subsequent printings of DSM—II would contain the new category and its explanatory paragraph.

Two psychiatrists displeased with the decision, Charles Socarides and Irving Bieber, circulated a petition demanding a referendum of the entire APA membership on this question. They secured the required number of signatures and the referendum was held in April 1974. With over 10,000 of the membership voting, the classification change was supported 58 percent to 42 percent. This decision has prompted gay groups to urge that the APA initiate new policies to protect the civil rights of homosexuals. Thus, a focus on systems of classification has provided a wedge in the conflict between psychiatric and gay definitions of homosexuality.

SOME RELATED LINES OF INVESTIGATIONS

In presenting these materials to illustrate the implications of a definitional approach to social problems, we have been very literal in our focus on how social conditions are defined. These materials also describe processes of definition in very pure form. They indicate, with as much precision as we are now able to provide, the type of documentation which is necessary to give substance to the notion that "social problems are inseparably joined to subjective awareness" as suggested by Nisbet.

Some work in sociology bears directly on how social problems are defined. Work in related areas, such as legislative histories, sheds light on the social construction of social problems. Laws that penalize or regulate an act, behavior, or condition can be carriers of alternative definitions. Excellent models exist which illustrate how legislatures participate in the process of definition. Becker (1963), Dickson (1968), Cook (1969), Reasons (1974), Galliher and Walker (1977), and Lindesmith (1965) have described the origins and development of prohibitions against marijuana. Roby (1969) and Holmes (1972) have written about prostitution, and Sutherland (1950a, b) has documented the diffusion of sexual psychopath laws.

Studies of the mass media also touch on the social construction of social problems. Recent writings have presented a view of news as "purposive behavior," that is, as activity that not only reacts to events, but creates them as well (Molotch and Lester, 1974). The media, by allocating personnel and time and space, funnel resources and attention to some activities and not to others. In so doing, decisions are made as to what will become news and what will not.

Many students of social movements and collective behavior believe that the image of protest groups in newspapers can influence the rate of growth of a movement by creating a specific picture of the organization in the eyes of potential recruits. Quite different conceptions are conveyed if a meeting of a women's liberation group is covered in the feature or family section of the newspaper, rather than in the front news section. Newspaper managing boards make decisions that systematically influence what subjects will appear in their papers. A decision to publish the daily pollution readings increases the exposure and publicity to this condition. The decision to create a "beat" may also further promote some problems at the expense of others. The creation of a pollution or environmental beat means some reporter will devote a considerable amount of time becoming knowledgeable on these issues, making contacts with pollution groups and environmental protection agencies, and have an inside track getting stories into the paper. Such efforts may insure that the press is informed well in advance of planned protest or enforcement activities and may mean that even when no particular "hot news" exists on the subject, background and feature stories will regularly appear, keeping the issue alive and before the public. Such decisions may also mean that pollution editors will develop some recognized expertise and become public figures or influential forces in policy determination.

Like all other groups that create categories and disseminate knowledge, information, or news to a larger public, the mass media may become the objects of complaints that the categories they use are morally objectionable. Thus, claims by various groups of unfair or biased coverage, or of blackouts and boycotts of stories, present competing definitions of what constitutes and should be reported as news. Similarly, sexually segregated help-wanted advertisements have been attacked on the grounds that they perpetuate sexist ideas and practices of sex discrimination in the job market. Most newspapers have discontinued segregating male and female job advertisements in spite of the fact, they say, that both the advertisers and those looking for jobs would prefer separate columns.

With the preceding examples, we have tried to show the thrust of the sociology of social problems that we shall elaborate in the pages that follow. They address what has been called the subjective approach to the study of social problems, in contrast to the objective approach that addresses the determinants of the "actual conditions" quite apart from how they are defined by members. This distinction between subjective and objective approaches equates the subjective with the ephemeral, or with elusive states of mind that sociologists are ill-equipped to study. On the contrary, the activities through which definitions of social problems are constructed are as observable through sociological research techniques as are any of the phenomena that occupy the attention of social scientists. It is therefore puzzling that the kinds of materials we have presented should be considered "subjective." All of these phenomena are observable, and the systems of categories and institutional procedures that constitute these social constructions of reality appear amenable to description and analysis.

2

Functional and Normative Definitions

This chapter reviews two ways that social problems are currently defined. One is the *functional approach,* which stresses the idea of social disorganization. The other is what we shall call the *normative approach,* which is characteristic of both the functional and more eclectic formulations. We will examine in detail the definitional statements of several authors and ask if these definitions are, in fact, implemented and reflected in their analyses of the empirical work they present.

Our analysis is conceptual and logical rather than historical. Some readers may find our discussions of definitions overly long and filled with excessive hair-splitting of semantic issues. Indeed, a recent critic (Westhues, 1973) of the literature observed that the sociology of social problems has come to be more concerned with what social scientists say than with the problems themselves. While this point is well taken, much of the confusion that clouds descriptions and analyses of social problems results from ambiguous, and often outright sloppy, definitional statements. We consider it essential to clarify the definitional issues in order to provide a theoretically defensible and empirically researchable subject matter.

THE FUNCTIONAL ETIOLOGICAL APPROACH

One theoretical approach has dominated the writings on social problems for over fifty years. The approach has been called by different names: what is now called social disorganization, or dysfunctionality, used to be called social pathology, just as deviant behavior used to be called personal disorganization. Stripped of fads and fashions, however, the core of the functional etiological approach is the following: identify conditions or behaviors that impede the fulfillment of society's goals, that interfere with the smooth functioning of society, or that throw society into disequilibrium. Having identified these as social problems, the functionalists seek to analyze and explain the origins of these conditions. Thus, a functional diagnosis of society is used to identify the subject matter of study, and an etiological theory is constructed to explain the conditions identified.

We shall use the term *functionalism* to refer to all varieties of this dominant tradition in social problems theory. This term is of relatively recent vintage and certainly was not used by early theorists or the writers who criticized them. During the 1920's the term *social pathology* was current, and in the 1930's the term *social disorganization* displaced it. The terms *function* (or "eufunction") and *dysfunction* have been popular since the 1950's. Thus when we say that Frank (1925) and Waller (1936) were critical of the functional view, we mean they were criticizing a theory that made what we call a functional argument. Although the early writers in this field would not have called their own writings functionalism, their statements reflected a common belief that social problems should be diagnosed by the sociologist as conditions that are destructive to society.

As an example of this theory to describe and criticize, we have chosen the most recent and most fully developed functional approach to social problems, written by the most prestigious, currently active functional theorist. We believe that this is superior to choosing an older work, which would suffer both from dated terminology and lack of exposure to current thinking about functional theory. When we say writers in the 1930's were critical of functional theory, it was, of course, not the present-day formulations they read and criticized, but the "disorganization" writers of their own day. It is our judgment that the current examples would have been no more satisfactory to those early critics.

The most elaborate application of functional theory to social problems is found in the epilogue to the third edition of *Contemporary Social Problems* (1971), by Robert K. Merton. Merton divides social problems into two broad categories—social disorganization and deviant behavior. This distinction is reflected in the organization of the book. One-half of the collected papers are presented as discussions of social disorganization, the other half as deviant behavior. The categories, however, are apparently not mutually exclusive types of social problems:

> *Even before we examine the theoretical basis for distinguishing these two classes of social problems, we can reasonably be sure that the two concepts are analytical, not depictive; abstract, not concrete. That is to say, they do not describe classes of events in all their actual complexity, but refer only to selected aspects of them. That is why we find in each of the concrete social problems examined in this book . . . evidence of both social disorganization and deviant behavior, though in differing compounds. (1971:818-819)*

The concepts of deviant behavior and social disorganization have been the objects of extensive commentary and criticism. The former, defined simply as the violation of institutionalized norms, has gained rather wide acceptance among sociologists. This definition, too, is not without its difficulties. Critics have asked, how are norms to be identified? How does the sociological observer determine when a norm is violated? What if no violation occurs, but members react as if there were a violation, or vice versa? Does that mean the sociologist was incorrect about what the norms were in the first place? And so on. The notion that deviant behavior may be defined with respect to norms requires assumptions about the normative integration of a society and some notion of value consensus. But it does not require a full-blown functional theory of social systems.

In contrast, the concept of social disorganization may be defined only within an elaborate set of assumptions and assertions, as expressed in the following statement by Merton:

> Social disorganization refers to inadequacies or failures in a social system of interrelated statuses and roles, such that the collective purposes and individual objectives of its members are less fully realized than they could be in an alternative workable system. . . . When we say that a particular group or organization or community or society is disorganized in some degree we mean that the structure of statuses and roles is not as effectively organized as it, then and there, might be. This type of statement, then, amounts to a technical judgment about the workings of a social system. And each case requires the sociological judge to supply competent evidence that the actual organization of social life can, under attainable conditions, be technically improved. (1971:820)

Merton goes on to indicate that social disorganization may be thought of as "representing inadequacies in meeting one or more of the functional requirements of the system." (1971:820)

Thus, in principle, the designation of a condition as social disorganization requires considerable groundwork, both theoretical and empirical. It requires that we assume our basic unit of analysis to be *a system* since disorganization is "the failure of a system." How may we draw the boundaries of the system, distinguishing what is inside from what is outside? What is the system in which, for example, an urban renewal project fails to satisfy the housing needs and demands of its residents? To call a particular institution or activity a system requires much theoretical specification and research.

The system itself is assumed to have collective purposes, since Merton speaks of the failure to achieve "collective purposes and individual objectives." What are the collective purposes of the system and who defines them? These are key elements of the definition of social disorganization, since we must assess failures in performance against some standards. These standards are particularly important in assessing the failure of the system. Any system may appear not to achieve its standards in view of particularly idealistic or perfectionist views of its collective purposes and individual objectives. Since these failures are a relative judgment of the sociological analyst, particular care is required in defining the standards by which to measure failure.

If social disorganizations are not only an indication that collective purposes "are less fully realized than they could be in an alternative workable system," but also "dysfunctions" within the system, then a more absolute judgement is logically required. The term *dysfunction* implies not only that some purposes are not being completely fulfilled, but also that some basic underpinnings of the system are not being maintained. In effect, the life or existence of the system is threatened. Conditions conceived to be necessary for the persistence of the system are called *functional prerequisites,* and a number of sociologists have devised lists and tables of them. Merton invokes the list devised by Parsons and Shils (1953:180-190), but allows that "whether this list of functional requirements or another is employed need not be at issue." (1971:821)

Any given condition that might be called a manifestation of social disorganization or a dysfunction may, of course, have multiple consequences. It may tend to support some institutions and undermine others. That is, it may be functional for some sectors of society and dysfunctional for other sectors. If the concept were to be taken seriously, the researcher would have to devise a means of making an over all assessment of the impact of a condition—tracing all of its consequences in all parts of a system—or of splitting up a system into subsystems according to the functional and dysfunctional impacts of the condition.

Finally, to apply the label of social disorganization, the sociological judge must not only show that the condition interferes with collective purposes and individual objectives and undermines some fundamental societal institution or support, she must also show that this *need not happen.* The sociologist must show in each instance that the society is not "as effectively organized as it then and there might be," and must also "supply competent evidence that the actual organization of social life can, under attainable conditions, be technically improved." Merton's comment on this concept is worth noting:

> *"A social dysfunction refers to a* designated *set of consequences of a* designated *pattern of behavior, belief, or organization that interferes with a* designated *functional requirement of a* designated *social system. Otherwise, the term social dysfunction becomes little more than an epithet of disparagement or a largely vacuous expression of attitude." (1971:839)*

This demand is surely the most difficult requirement to meet. It is one thing to argue that goals are not being met or that some condition is distasteful or injurious to some class of people. It is quite another to supply competent evidence that things need not be that way.

Since all definitions are to some degree arbitrary, how may we judge whether this is a good definition of social disorganization and, in turn, a useful approach to the study of social problems? While all definitions have arbitrary aspects, none of the elements or assertions contained in a definition are true *by definition.* Each requires argument, support, and documentation. Do countries, states, counties, and cities warrant the title of system? They do not become systems just by being called systems; the designation requires empirical support. So does the assertion that systems in general, or any particular system, have collective purposes. And how is a list of functional prerequisites of a system to be evaluated? Surely, the validity of such a list or any item in it is not determined by the assertion of any social scientist. When the sociologist supplies "competent evidence of a technical nature," what are the bases for the assertion that the evidence is technical and not ideological, competent and not incompetent, and who is to make such judgments?

We have discussed the methodological problems posed by the functionalist definition of social disorganization. While Merton discusses these issues as if they were matters of definition, each is actually a hypothesis—an empirical question. For any given condition—crime, poverty, community conflict, pollution, suicide, drug addiction, automation, or divorce—to be classified as social disorganization, the sociological analyst must supply evidence that it meets the requirements specified by the functionalist conception of social systems. Assuming that the adherents of the social disorganization theory are aware of the full implications of their formulation, they have set a task of immense proportions for themselves. As Merton himself acknowledges:

> *. . . to find such evidence is no easy task. This is why, perhaps, diagnoses of social disorganization are often little more than moral judgments, rather than confirmable technical judgments about the workings of a social system. (1971:820)*

We have argued for the importance of a theoretically defensible, methodologically specifiable, and empirically researchable definition of social problems. Our examination of the literature leads us, as well as other commentators, to conclude that authors of social problems texts present their definition of the subject matter in an obligatory way, then fail to apply and document its use in their selection of topics and content. Why would these authors go to the trouble of constructing a definition—often a very elaborate, ambitious, and even pretentious definition—and then fail to use it, or even give the appearance of applying it? A brief discussion of the development of social problems as a concept and as an area of sociological investigation may provide an answer to this question.

Several writers suggest that the functional or, as it was called earlier, social pathology theory of social problems was not a delineation of a subject matter for serious and systematic investigation. Rather, it was a response to the low repute of sociological writings and the sociologists' dependence on other disciplines and professions for both facts and theories.

The theoretical phase of the ordinary study usually—and in most cases fortunately—has been confined to the opening section of the book as a kind of ceremony that must be observed before settling down to business. (Martindale, 1957:358)

Richard Fuller, a major critic of the functionalist view and the principal proponent of the value-conflict approach, described the growth of the pathology theory:

This process of delimiting a sociological theory of pathology was accompanied by increased demands for objectivity in sociology. Much of the criticism of the teaching of social problems up to this time rested in the charge of professional fakery; i.e., the sociologist took his information and ideas from all other sciences and then proceeded to pass moral judgment on what ought to be done. Hence, it is not surprising that sociologists interested in social problems welcomed a distinctly sociological point of view, and they studiously took care of the accusation of bias by emphasizing their personal detatchment from the problem they considered. (Fuller, 1938:416)

Both authors see the rise of pathology theory in the study of social problems more as a response to external evaluations of the young, low-caste discipline of sociology than as part of the intellectual project of defining a researchable subject matter. We shall not digress further in this analysis except to quote the personal reminiscence of a sociologist describing the period during the 1930's when functional theory came to dominate social problems textbooks:

As you no doubt learned in your first course on the history of sociology, American sociologists of the first two decades of this century were—with some few exceptions, of which Cooley is the only one that immediately comes to mind—mere moralistic reformers in scientific clothing. What you may not know, or at least not fully appreciate, is that well into the 1930's the status of sociology, and hence of sociologists was abominable, both within and outside the academic community. The public image of the sociologist was that of a bluenosed reformer, ever ready to pronounce moral judgments, and against all pleasurable forms of social conduct. . . . The men who were to shape sociology during the 1930's were, for the most part, products of one- or two-man departments of low status within their university. They were, therefore, to a considerable degree self-trained and without a doctrinaire viewpoint, and they were exceedingly conscious of the low esteem in which sociology was held.

Such men, and I was among them, were determined to prove—at least to themselves—that sociology is a science, that sociologists are not moral-

ists, and that sociology deserves recognition and support comparable to that being given psychology and economics. (Richard LaPierre, quoted in Deutscher, 1973:36-37)

LaPierre goes on to say that sociologists turned to statistics and quantitative methods in order to gain prestige and the appearance of scientific rigor. They also created grand theories, of which the functional formulation of social problems is a direct descendant. LaPierre's comments suggest that the search for academic respectability shaped the development of the functional perspective. We shall not pursue this analysis except to mention another, perhaps rival, commentary on the same writings. C. Wright Mills (1940), in a now classic discussion of the early social problems literature, argued that many sociologists in the 1940's were recent arrivals to the large northern cities, and that their conceptions of the society that confronted them as disorganized reflected their application of homogeneous, rural and small-town ideals to the heterogeneity of big-city life. Thus, while LaPierre points to the importance of projected ambitions in the fashioning of functional theory, Mills suggests that past experiences also produced the same theoretical perspective.

Martindale (1957) proposed that the functionalist definitions of social problems might be considered "ceremonies" intended to attract the attention of and suitably impress an audience of academic colleagues and followers. Disorganization writers usually confine their attention to this theory to the introductions and conclusions of their books. None of the contributors to Merton and Nisbet's volume seriously attempt to confront the arguments and documentations required by the definition of social disorganization. Richard Fuller's evaluation of the contribution of functional theory to the teaching of social problems applies today as it did almost forty years ago:

The student may well ask what this theory contributes to the sociological knowledge of [concrete] problems. The instructor has two alternatives: he may relegate the preliminary theory to the role of window-dressing and proceed to a discussion of the real goods which make up the problem, or he can fake his way along by making an artificial and stilted analysis within the preconceived theoretical frame. (1938:417)

The conclusion that the social disorganization theory produced no empirical research is not true. A sizable empirical literature exists that invokes this name, most notably that of the "Chicago school" (Faris, 1967). These writings still interest contemporary students of social conditions in urban society. However, their value largely lies in their description of the organization of institutions rather than in their claims that these institutions are disorganized. Painstaking ethnographies of institutions, such as the taxi-dance hall (Cressey, 1932), depicted the variety and detail of community life. In contrast, the introductions and conclusions of these studies, where the case for social disorganization is argued, seem theoretically inconsistent, out of date, and strangely moralistic.

David Matza (1969) has thoughtfully analyzed this strain in social disorganization research:

> *How describe the fact of diversity in urban America yet maintain the idea of pathology? That was the Chicago dilemma. . . . The Chicagoans based their resolution on the ubiquity of social organization. Society was composed of rules and roles that were organized or welded into coherent and usable form. Despite their familiarity with deviant roles and eccentric rules, they clung to the idea that social organization was equivalent to more or less conventional social organization. . . .*

> *Since the Chicagoans were intimate enough with their subjects to observe and describe the social organization of deviant life, and since they conceived of peculiar worlds, a question regarding the possibility of the integrity and autonomy of such worlds must have arisen. But to face such a question would have amounted to grappling with and actually resolving the choice between pathology and diversity. By conceiving of social disorganization, the Chicagoans avoided a resolution. . . . Thus the antithetical ideas persisted side by side. The tension between them never resolved, a neat division emerged: pathology was conceived and diversity described. The taxi-dance hall, say, was described in infinite detail, but the reality of that phenomenon was cast in a moral framework that rendered it pathological. . . .*

> *The Chicagoans left the idea of pathology in a tenuous state. While maintaining it in their concept of social disorganization, they weakened it by the attention they devoted to the facts of diversity, especially the social organization of deviant life. (1969:45ff)*

As Matza argues, there were strong differences between what disorganization researchers actually did in their research and what they said they were doing in their more theoretical and interpretive writings. We have paid more attention to the latter and thus risk misrepresenting their overall effort. On the other hand, the fact that social disorganization research largely stands on its own without the concept of disorganization does not encourage us to make that concept the basis of a sociology of social problems. We agree with Matza that the Chicago school achieved its considerable vigor in research in spite of, rather than because of, the concept of social disorganization.

THE NORMATIVE APPROACH

Although the disorganization theory asserts that the classification of social conditions as social problems is technical rather than ideological, critics have charged that value judgments are simply disguised as factual assessments of conditions. This charge has been the basis for a continuing debate on the role of values in the definition and analysis of social problems. Martindale comments as follows:

> *Crime rings, for example, are treated as examples of disorganization. Yet they are often more "organized" than the society in which they appear, and in which they are assumed to represent "disorganization." Clearly normative judgments, in these instances, are being disguised as factual judgments. Crime rings are not objected to because they are examples of disequilibrium, but because they are normatively objectionable. (1957:358)*

The criterion by which crime rings are called social problems is not the technical diagnosis of disorganization, but the implicit judgment that crime rings violate normative standards. The use of such normative standards as the basis for defining social problems is a strategy found in a variety of formulations. It is prevalent in functionalist writings, but it occurs in nonfunctional and more eclectic theories as well. While it is not surprising that functional theories relying heavily on a value consensus model should use norms and values as the basis for defining social problems, the difficulties posed by this strategy are quite different from those posed by diagnoses of social disorganization. Therefore, while Merton's formulation provided the model for our previous discussion, his definitions also rely on normative standards, and we again draw on his work in the current section.

The use of norms to define social problems is not limited to the functional approach. Its major rival, the value-conflict approach, which we treat in detail in the next chapter, also uses consensus-based concepts to define social problems. As we examine their definitions side by side, we illustrate that while the two positions are antithetical in many ways, in one important respect they display virtually identical difficulties.

The two definitions follow. The first is by critics of the functionalist approach, and the second, the most recent statement of that approach:

> *A social problem is a condition which is defined by a considerable number of persons as a deviation from some social norm which they cherish. (Fuller and Myers, 1941a:320)*

A social problem is a substantial discrepancy between widely shared social standards and actual conditions of social life. (Merton, 1971:799)

Both definitions attempt to identify social problems directly and not through an intermediary concept, as in the case of social disorganization or deviant behavior. Both definitions make clear that the normative standards are not those of the sociologist-reformers using their own personal prejudice to determine theoretical categories. Both imply that social problems are conditions defined by members of a society as social problems, and that it is the task of the sociologist to measure, monitor, or assess this process. The primary task in the implementation of these definitions is *methodological* in contrast to the *conceptual* difficulties inherent in the idea of dysfunctions and disorganization.

In the first case, the key phrase is "considerable number." In order to implement this definition, we must ask, how many is considerable? We have to know this in order to classify conditions as social problems. If this quantitative criterion is to play a key role in the most primitive definition of the subject matter, some rule or number must be calculated and justified for application to all cases of social problems; or alternatively, we must determine for each separate case how many people constitute a "considerable number." This problem follows directly from the reference to "numbers of persons." To refer to a number of people invites the question, "How many?"

The definition also requires that the term "persons define the condition as a problem" be specified. What consitutes the activity of defining a condition as a problem is not immediately observable. The term must be translated into a set of procedures for identifying and documenting behavior that defines a condition as a social problem. Would this consist of holding an opinion about a given condition or expressing that opinion in a Gallup Poll? Writing an angry letter to a member of Congress or organizing a protest? Committing an act of self-immolating martyrdom?

In the second definition, the key phrase is "widely shared." While it makes no explicit reference to numbers of people, concepts based on consensus provide its foundation. We need only to ask, "How widely shared must the standard be? Which and how many people must share it to meet the condition 'widely shared'?" It is apparent that the same methodological problems plague this definition. Note that we do not deny there are widely shared social standards. If that term were properly defined, we might well conclude that substantial agreement existed on a variety of issues, although an empirical argument would be required for each case.

Our objection to Fuller and Myers' and Merton's definitions rests on theoretical, rather than empirical grounds. Are assertions about widely shared social standards a fruitful way to build a sociology of social problems? On the evidence of fifty years of social problems textbooks, we think the answer is probably not. While many authors have espoused consensus-based definitions of social problems, we know of none that have seriously attempted to apply them. Rather, the practice is to present such definitions and then ignore them.

Merton is more sensitive than most to the problem of specifying which and how many people must define a condition as a social problem. Under the subheading "The Judges of Social Problems," the following categories of people are all identified as recognizing social problems in Merton's discussion:

> the majority of people (p. 806)
>
> problem definers (p. 806)
>
> various categories of men in society (p. 808)
>
> those occupying strategic positions of authority and power (p. 803)
>
> a functionally significant collectivity (p. 817)

If we add the categories of people identified by Merton's coeditor, Robert Nisbet, in his introductory chapter to the same volume, the list includes:

> a substantial part of a social order (p. 1)
>
> large numbers of people (p. 3)
>
> a determining number of the American people (p. 12)

All of these refer to somewhat different categories of individuals, although they seem to be used interchangeably. None is easily operationalized, i.e., translated into procedures for determining exactly how many and which people must define a condition or recognize it as a problem. For example, who does Merton think are those who "occupy strategic positions of authority and power"? Are they elected officials? Corporation executives and board members who "control" the legislators? Such substantive issues must be addressed if the "large numbers" or "significant segments" approach to the definition of social problems is chosen. The phrase "functionally significant collectivity" is simply no substitute for an operational specification of such a collectivity.

Ironically, the use of an explicitly quantitative concept has prevented, rather than insured, precision and rigor in the definition of social problems. While the concept permits one to think in terms of a continuum from everyone to no one, the methodological problems of translating this variable into a scale of measurement are insurmountable. Since concepts such as values, goals, and norms share the same consensus base as standards, all definitions of social problems as conditions discrepant from society's values harbor the problems discussed here. In the case of Merton's definition, which contains the dubious assumption that the sociologist can assess the "actual conditions of social life," there appears to be no prospect of measuring the discrepancies alluded to unless the numbers problem can be resolved.

Skolnick and Currie (1970) have noted this ambiguity in Merton's definition:

> *Merton's approach is best seen as providing a rationale for evaluating and criticizing particular policies and structures within a presumable consensual society whose basic values and directions are not seen as problematic. . . .* It is never clear whether he merely reflects or helps to shape those "socially shared standards," nor is it at all clear just whose standards they are. *(1970:11-13) (Emphasis added.)*

Merton makes two points in response to this criticism. First, he quotes five brief fragments from his own writings which mention that different strata and groups have distinctive interests and values. Second, he countercharges that his critics, Skolnick and Currie, who would change and reform social institutions, "must assume, just as the functional orientation does, *some* degree of consensus among *some* people." (1971:790) His denial of the charge leveled at his definition is highly qualified, and he makes no effort to translate "some consensus among some people" into more concrete terms. In our view, Merton is correct in pointing to the implications of Skolnick and Currie's position, which leads us to underscore our point that all such assumptions of consensus are poor bases for developing a sociology of social problems. Although Skolnick and Currie propose to "radicalize" the sociology of social problems, their formulation with its implicit assumption of a value consensus among segments of the society is burdened with the same methodological problems discussed previously.

Both normative approaches assume that the definition of conditions as problems is a "member's activity"; that is, it is an activity carried out by the members of a society, not one performed by expert observers such as sociologists. The sociologist's role is not to identify which social problems exist in the society, but to monitor what "the consensus" indicates them to be. If some people define a condition as a problem in society, presumably the sociologist must abide by what they say and think. What the sociologist should observe is not the condition, but how people act in relation to it. The sociologist could not simply observe the condition and decide if it were a social problem. Some sociologists have found it difficult to accept this passive role.

> *This definition more or less identifies sociologists with the lay populace and makes public opinion sociological opinion, with implied faith in a democratic process. Its difficulties accrue from recognition of the irrational or spurious qualities in public expressions or collective behavior, which counsels considerable discounting of public reactions or moral indignation as guides for sociological criticism of society or its institutions . . . the subjectivism inherent in the "popular" definition of social problems runs athwart the conception of sociology as a body of knowledge which*

rises above common sense, and is accumulated through application of special methods by observers or researchers at least relatively detached from the social facts under scrutiny. If some social problems are defined in terms of such a body of knowledge, they become objective, rather than subjective facts, "discoverable" from laws or generalizations about necessary conditions of social life. (Lemert, 1968:454-455; see also Manis, 1974a)

Thus, not only do "irrational or spurious qualities" mar "popular" definitions of social problems, they also pose a threat to the sociologist's status as objective scientist investigating the etiology of social conditions.

Merton shares this assessment of members' definitions of social problems. While he refers to "widely shared social standards" (presumably shared by ordinary members of the society) he refuses to limit the subject matter of the sociology of social problems to popular definitions.

For the sociologist to confine himself only to the conditions in society that a majority of people regard as undesirable, would be to exclude study of all manner of other conditions that are in fact at odds with the declared values of those who accept these conditions. . . . For not all conditions and processes of society inimical to the values of men are recognized as such by them. (1971:806)

Merton proposes a solution that acknowledges the relevance of "people's definitions" while reserving for the sociologist the knowledge and capacity to identify social problems of which people are *not* aware. This solution is presented in his distiction between manifest and latent social problems.

It is the function of the sociologist to discover and to report the human consequences of holding to certain values and practices, just as it is his function to discover and to report the human consequences of departing from these values and practices. Apart from manifest social problems— those objective social conditions identified by problem-definers as at odds with social values—are latent social problems, conditions that are also at odds with values current in society, but are not generally recognized as being so. (1971:806)

Two issues are at stake in this distinction. One is the limitation of the sociologist to social problems as they are defined by the people, a position Merton characterizes as "heedless subjectivism" and "a self-deceiving guise." The second is a claim that sociologists have expertise enough to disagree with popular definitions when they judge that certain conditions are "at odds with values current in the society." Let us first examine the implications of the distinction between manifest and latent social problems. Fundamentally, this distinction contends that in some instances the members' definitions are to be accepted as the basis for identifying a social problem, but in other instances they are not. The possibilities may be presented schematically in a fourfold table.

Sociologist's Definition

		Social Problem	*No Social Problem*
		(1)	(2)
	Social Problem	"Manifest" Social Problem	"Spurious" Social Problem
		(3)	(4)
	No Social Problem	"Latent" Social Problem	"Normal" Social Condition

(Row label, vertical: **Members' Definition**)

Merton's position appears to be that when the sociologists and members of a society disagree on whether there is "a substantial discrepancy between expectations and actuality," the sociologists' definition, being based on objective evidence, takes precedence. The cases at issue where sociologists and members disagree are represented in Cells 2 and 3 in the table. In Cell 2, which might be called spurious social problems as perceived by the sociologist, are cases where there is "much ado about nothing." In Cell 3 there is *no* ado about *something,* again from the sociologist's point of view. From the member's perspective, of course, these labels would be reversed.

There are three components in Merton's definition: (a) sociologists and members may agree or disagree in assessing the conditions; (b) they may agree or disagree in determining the socially shared standards relevant to those conditions; (c) finally, when they are agreed on both of the above, they may agree or disagree as to whether or not a discrepancy exists between conditions and social standards.

In assessing the actual conditions of a society, sociologists might disagree with members of a society, but only reluctantly and after careful analysis. Sociological research may result in different assessments of a condition than a common sense view taken by members, a difference the sociologist might suggest is due to the laymen's lack of technical training or inability to interpret the significance of what they observe. But surely sociologists are on weaker ground if they disagree with members about what are their values or socially shared standards, or which particular value or standard is to be applied to a given condition. (Sociologists have only begun to scratch the methodological surface in their efforts to assess and measure values. For a recent and ambitious work on this subject, see Rokeach, 1968.) Here sociologists are very dependent on the opinions and statements of members. This being so, on what basis may sociologists disagree with members about their values?

Merton avoids or ignores this question, for he directly follows his definition of manifest and latent social problems with the following statement:

> *The sociologist does not impose his values upon others when he undertakes to* supply knowledge *about latent social problems. (1971:806) (Emphasis added.)*

This, of course, passes over the prior question of whether sociologists impose their own values in identifying conditions as latent problems in the first place. If the members' definitions of some social conditions may be accepted as the basis for identifying some social problems (manifest) but not others (latent), on what basis is the sociologist to make these discriminations? Following the logic of Merton's argument, members must accept the sociologist's standards, or his view of their standards, in order for a social problem to be manifest. Thus, all social problems would become manifest when all members share the sociologist's standards and perceive the "actual conditions of social life" with the same degree of accuracy and perspicacity.

The rhetoric in which these claims for the sociologist's superior knowledge and judgment are set reveals a professional ideology. Merton states:

> *Through its successive uncovering of latent social problems and through its clarification of manifest social problems, sociological inquiry does make men increasingly accountable for the outcome of their collective and institutionalized actions. (1971:808)*

This theme also emerges in the introduction by Merton's coeditor, Robert Nisbet. Declaring that "nothing could be more false than the occasional charge that sociologists are indifferent to moral standards," Nisbet goes on to assert:

> *The social scientist is interested in making the protection of society his first responsibility, in seeing society reach higher levels of moral decency, and, when necessary, in promoting such legal actions as are necessary, in the short run for protection or decency. (1971:20)*

The seemingly innocuous assertion that the scope of the sociologists' investigations is not limited by popular definitions and evaluations of social conditions in fact hides an ideological and highly questionable role: the sociologist as the conscience and protector of society.

WHOSE NORMATIVE STANDARDS?

The functionalist and normative definitions of social problems continue to reflect implicitly the values that shape the sociologists' assessments of social conditions. There is certainly no question that the earliest social problems texts were written by outspoken reformers and crusaders who made no secret of their own commitments or the fact that they advocated a value position. A later generation of sociologists was embarrassed by this legacy and invented theories that did not require them to be value committed or to play the role of the bluenosed reformer. Theories of disorganization are presented as value-neutral and objective; theories using normative definitions carefully specify that social problems are conditions that violate society's standards and values, not those of the sociologist.

Yet critics of these formulations have suggested that the values of the sociologist are still the guiding force behind the definitions, now disguised behind a facade of science. Martindale pointedly criticized disorganization theory as a normative theory, by which he meant it is a theory of what ought to be. Merton's distinction between manifest and latent problems documents Martindale's contention, since it explicitly sets aside the norms and values of the members of society in favor of the sociologist's diagnosis of social conditions. In addition, statements about the role of the sociologist as protector of society suggest that the reformer spirit still lives in the sociology of social problems.

CONCLUSION

The perspectives we discuss and develop in the remainder of the book are in part a reaction to the approaches presented and analyzed above. It is important to point out, however, that we do not reject the functional and normative approaches to social problems on the grounds that they have been discredited by empirical research, or that the formulation we present provides a better approach for the study of the same phenomenon. As a "grand" theoretical perspective, the functionalist view cannot be proven right or wrong. It is a way of viewing the world, of writing sociology, and of looking for intellectual projects and research questions. Objections to it must be taken as matters of taste, theoretical preferences, research strategies, or politics.

The functional approach never developed a distinctive concept of social problems. Instead, the study of social problems was assimilated into functional analysis, emphasizing dysfunctions and disorganization. The concept *social problems* was never made to refer to a distinctive set of conditions, processes, or activities. The application of the term to conditions identified as dysfunctional is simply redundant. For is anything added to the study of

deviant behavior by calling it a social problem? Do we increase our understanding of crime or poverty by pointing out that it is a social problem? Do
drug addiction, racism, divorce, pollution, war, and community disorganization have anything in common such that they may usefully be grouped in
the same category? We think not. To state the matter differently,even if the
functional formulation were taken seriously and rigorously apply to empirical
research, it would not produce a sociology of social problems, but only a
sociology of social disorganization, an explanation of social conditions, but
not of social problems.

In the same way, we do not reject the normative approach because it
has been proven wrong but because it has not produced a logically coherent
formulation for the study of social problems. Consensus-based concepts do
not easily translate into sensible operational definitions. There will always be
a "numbers game" of asking how many people must believe or do this or
that in order for the researcher to decide if a norm, a consensus, or a value
exists. Social problems should be defined without reference to the numbers of
people involved. Thus, our formulation will not offer a set of rival explanations for a commonly defined subject matter. We argue for a different
subject matter for the sociology of social problems.

Although the approach we shall attempt to delineate is in part a
criticism and reaction to the functionalist view, one may not decide between
them on empirical grounds. The two approaches produce rival conceptions
of social problems and thus subject matter; they direct us to different lines
of investigation.

Our aim in this book is to develop as clearly as possible an approach to
social problems that does the following:

1. Defines the phenomenon, the subject matter for analysis, in a clear and
   unambiguous manner that is amendable to empirical investigation.
2. Justifies the addition of the new conceptual category "social problems"
   by distinguishing its content from that of other previously defined or
   related categories.

In the next chapter we discuss a group of writers who began to create a
distinctive sociology of social problems. After reviewing their efforts, we
present our own elaboration of this view.

3

The Value-Conflict School

Beginning in the 1920's several sociologists, dissatisfied with the prevailing conception of social problems, contended that the most important element that distinguishes social problems as a sociological phenomenon—namely the value judgments of the members of society—was systematically excluded from study. They argued that in the absence of such judgments, a given social condition cannot be differentiated from any other *as a social problem*. We will examine the implications of this view of social problems and the definitions it has produced.

While the functionalist conception of social problems firmly dominated the textbooks in the 1920's and 1930's, a number of sociologists dissented from the approach in scholarly journals. Criticism of functional theory was their point of departure, and it is clear they wrote defensively, in reaction to perceived inadequacies in the concepts of pathology and disorganization. The mutual antagonism between these critics and those sponsoring the dominant approach to social problems is seen in an exchange of comments published as a discussion of a paper by Richard Fuller, "The Problem of Teaching Social Problems." Among the discussants were several representatives of the dominant view: John Gillen, Stuart Queen, and Mabel Elliot.

Gillen, in particular, was critical of the paper, belittling Fuller's effort as mere semantics and concept mongering, and asserting that social problems research is about "just what conditions in our contemporary civilization do actually prevent the smooth working of our social organization" (Fuller, 1938:427). In reply, Fuller made explicit his dissatisfaction with the concept of social disorganization:

> *The hypothesis of a smooth-functioning social order is not only artificial, but dangerous.... We must abandon the notion that social problems represent human behavior which is a departure from an unquestioned and smooth-running cultural status quo.... When did economic institutions ever function in perfect efficiency? When was religious dogma ever allowed to go unchallenged? Was there ever a time*

without confused and confounded individuals? And when did the nations of the world live in harmony? In other words, when and where do we sociologists find this nice equilibrium of forces (social organization) from which we are supposed to be slipping into a morass of confusion (social disorganization)? (1938:433-434)

In constructing their own definitions of social problems, the value-conflict theorists sought to distinguish between an objective condition and the definition of conditions as a problem. Clarence Case, in 1924, was the first author to insist that no objective condition, however adverse, could itself constitute a social problem:

A social problem means any social situation which attracts the attention of a considerable number of competent observers within a society, and appeals to them as calling for readjustment or remedy by social, i.e., collective action of some kind or other. (1924:268)

The essential feature of this definition is its socio-psychological *character, That is to say, a "social problem" is not a purely objective situation, which can be recognized by a stranger, no matter how proficient in the social sciences. . . . A social "problem" is partly a state of the social mind, and hence not purely a matter of unfavorable objective conditions in the physical or social environment. An expert statistician or social worker may be perfectly competent to point out the existence and nature, and even the causes and remedies in some cases, of* adverse social conditions *in any society on earth, but neither he, nor any other outsider, can single out the* social problems *of a social group, except by studying the* collective mind *of that group. (1924:269)*

Note that Case's definition, with its reference to "competent observers within a society," bears a similarity to the observers implied in Merton's "widely shared social standards." It shares the "numbers," "who," and "how many" problem that we discussed in the preceding chapter. Case was more explicitly aware of these difficulties than others who emphasized the subjective element of social problems. He followed his definition with an apology:

The phrase "considerable number" is confessedly vague, but is chosen deliberately to indicate any number, from a vast majority to a small minority, if capable and energetic. (1924:268)

He hints that the required number is an empirical question, and that sometimes a small, but well-organized and vigorous minority may succeed in defining a condition as a problem. His main point is that social problems are subjective states and require analysis of the "collective mind" of the group.

Willard Waller, more than a decade later, echoed and elaborated the position of Case. He rejected the disorganization approach even more dramatically and insisted on the subjective nature of social problems:

> *Various attempts to treat social problems in a scientific manner have proved useless because they have dealt only with the objective side of social problems, and have failed to include* the attitude which constituted them problems. *(Emphasis added.)*

> *Two errors . . . vitiate the work of those who have tried to deal with social problems scientifically. (A) In attempting to exclude value judgments from their discussion, they have unwittingly ruled out the essential criterion by which social problems may be identified. (B) Having first ruled out the only thing which all social problems have in common, writers then endeavor vainly to find some other principle which will enable them to treat all social problems together. . . .*

> *Social problems exist within a definite moral universe. Once we step out of our circle of accustomed moralities, social problems cease to exist for us. . . . The existence of some sort of moral problem is the single thread that binds all social problems together. . . . Value judgments are the formal causes of social problems, just as the law is the formal cause of crime. (1936:922-925)*

Fuller and Myers extended this line of argument further and their rejection of the social disorganization theory contained the promise of a radically different approach:

> *Conditions do not assume a prominent place in a social problem until a given people define them as hostile to their welfare. . . . If the people are not problem-conscious, they will not behave as if there were any problem. They will not debate the condition as a problem, nor will they organize or do anything about it. . . . It is not enough that people are being or will be affected by objective conditions. Their behavior must indicate that they think the condition threatens cherished values. (1941a:25-26)*

> Social problems are what people think they are *and if conditions are not defined as social problems by the people involved in them, they are not problems to those people, although they may be problems to outsiders or to scientists. (1941b—320)*

We have quoted at length from the early proponents of the value-conflict approach to demonstrate their intent to create a sociology of social problems radically different from the dominant functionalist formulation. They appear to say that social problems are definitions constructed by members of a society, and that these constructions are expressions of value judgments. Definitions of conditions as social problems are the accomplishments of the members of a society.

Stated in this way, the sociologist should seek to identify the causes and antecedents of *the definitions* of social problems, not of the imputed objective conditions. The disinction repeatedly made in the preceding quotations between social conditions and the definitions of those conditions reflected this change in emphasis. The causes of the condition, or variations in the condition, are entirely different from the causes of the definition or variation in the definition. Furthermore, the *definition of the condition is not caused by the condition* in any meaningful sense.

Let us briefly illustrate this point. For a number of years the official definition of marijuana included the notion that is was not only dangerous, but addictive as well. This was reflected both in the official classification of the drug in legislation and in the medical literature, where the marijuana user was referred to as an addict. At a later date, marijuana was removed from the addiction classification, and the medical literature no longer referred to the pot smoker as an addict. (In an intermediate stage, some tried to argue for the concept of psychological addiction.) We presume that it is not the case that during the 1930's marijuana was addictive, but physiological changes occurred sometime during the 1960's to alter its effects on body chemistry; there is nothing in the nature of marijuana itself to explain this definitional change. The nature of marijuana remained constant throughout the interval and, therefore, an explanation of the variation in definition must come from another source. In fact, its "nature" cannot adequately explain either the definition of marijuana as an addictive or nonaddictive substance. The explanation of either definition must be sought in the conceptions held by various groups, the notion of addiction they applied, the type of evidence they used to support their views, the political strategies and tactics they used to gain acceptance of their definitions, and the support given them by governmental agencies for institutionalizing those definitions.

When the amount, distribution, or intensity of a condition does vary, the same logic applies: changes in conditions do not explain changes in definitions. When we consider statements about the *extent,* or "seriousness," as distinct from the *kind* of condition, a variety of examples might be presented to document the variability and plasticity of the relation between subjective definitions and the postulated conditions.

As an example of the literature that is relevant to this point, one study in diagnostic medicine examined how doctors are predisposed to see illness where "there is none." The study focused on the decision to remove the tonsils of a child. One thousand children were chosen for the study:

Some 611 had already had their tonsils removed. The remaining 389 were then examined by other physicians and 174 were selected for tonsillectomy. This left 125 children whose tonsils were apparently normal. Another group of doctors was put to work examining these 125 children, and 99 of them were adjudged in need of tonsillectomy. Still another group of doctors was then employed to examine the remaining children and nearly one-half were recommended for operation. (quoted in Freidson, 1970:257)

The experimental design makes it unlikely that an explanation may be found in the characteristics of the children, nor in changes of the condition of their tonsils between progressive examinations. Rather, the propensity of doctors to perceive, interpret, and define conditions as indications of illness and recommend treatment would seem an important explanatory element. [See Scheff (1966) for a discussion of the same professional ideology in psychiatric diagnoses of mental illness.]

These two examples indicate the logic that Fuller and Myers, Waller, and Case appear to be recommending. Their rejection of the social disorganization approach was clear enough, and their emphasis on the members' definitions of conditions, as opposed to the conditions themselves, promised to open up a new line of development, a line we propose to explore in subsequent chapters.

INCONSISTENCIES IN THE VALUE-CONFLICT POSITION

The value-conflict proponents did not pursue the line of inquiry indicated above. Instead, they reintroduced the concept of objective conditions into their formulation and obscured the originality and distinctiveness of the approach. They failed to shed the burden of the conventional (functional) formulation in spite of the fact that their point of departure was an explicit rejection of it.

It will be instructive to examine in some detail the failures and compromises of the value-conflict writings. Some of the inconsistencies in these writings may be viewed, perhaps, as conscious compromises in which the authors attempted to take a balanced and reasonable position and thus avoid a complete rupture from the conventional formulation. Thus, Fuller and Myers, who articulated the most extreme subjective definition of social problems, prepared the ground for "social problems are what people think they are" with these introductory statements:

Every social problem thus consists of an objective condition and a subjective definition. The objective condition is a verifiable situation which can be checked as to existence and magnitude (proportions) by

*impartial and trained observers. The subjective definition is the aware-
ness of certain individuals that the condition is a threat to certain
cherished values. . . . The objective condition is necessary, but not in
itself sufficient to constitute a social problem. (1941b:320)*

*Sociologists must, therefore, study not only the objective condition
phase of a social problem, but also the value-judgments of the people
involved in it which cause them to define the same condition and means
to its solution in different ways. (1941b:321)*

These statements clearly represent a retreat from Waller's position that
attitudes constituted the condition as a problem, and his implication that
the subjective definition was sufficient for the identification of a social
problem. In Fuller and Myers' statement, the definition alone is not
sufficient; an objective condition is necessary, but not in itself sufficient.

The ambiguity this introduces in the value-conflict formulation undercuts
the distinctive focus on the definitional process, independent of *what* those
definitions might be about. When the subjective definition is said to be
"the awareness that the condition is a threat," it is not clear whether the
term "awareness" (rather than "belief" or "conviction") was meant to
imply that the condition is *in fact* such a threat. This implication leads the
sociologist back to the position of the social disorganization theorist who
looks for the adverse consequences of objective conditions. However, when
the subjective definition is based on a *belief* that the condition is a threat,
the sociologist need not verify the existence of the imputed condition or make
an independent assessment of that condition.

Although this point may appear to be a minor, hairsplitting exercise in
semantics, it is, in fact, just such small compromises that confuse and
confound the logic of the value-conflict formulation. It is one thing to
study how individuals or groups construct a definition of a condition and
decide that it is a threat to them. It is quite another to ask how or whether
individuals or groups become aware of situations that are in fact threatening to them. The former focuses entirely on what the members of society do
and promises a delimited and homogeneous subject matter. The latter
requires an elaborate and far-reaching definition of what conditions "really
are," what people's interests "really are," and how an observer could
determine when those conditions constitute a "real threat."

These compromises draw attention away from the definitional process.
They reduce the members' perspectives in the definition of social problems
to the status of reactions to threats—mere reflex actions to the condition
itself. Some threats are recognized and some are not, which leads logically to
the question: how is it that some threatening conditions are recognized and
others are not? The independent significance of the definitional process fades
from sight, and with it the conception of threat as a members' construction that logically should be the object of inquiry.

The shift away from analysis of the definitional process is even more apparent and consequential in the typologies that Case and Fuller and Myers constructed of social problems. If social problems are definitions, then a typology of social problems should refer to kinds of definitions and explain their meanings or content. In a recent statement, Freidson proposed such a classification system of social meanings. He warned against the presumption that these meanings reflect and measure aspects of objective reality to which they make reference.

> *Given the fact that I am concerned with the social nature of deviance, the scheme will not be based on the bio-physical attributes of individuals, or on the acts to which meaning is attributed. Thus, it will not be based on the physical signs by which a physician diagnoses a disease, or on the proven offenses by which a judge or jury determines crime. Instead, the classification will be based on the meanings that people impute to physical attributes or concrete acts, whether or not the imputation is, in the professional view of doctors and judges, "correct." By such a tactic we liberate ourselves from the imperfect medicine and law of our and others' time without precluding the possibility of using their meanings, should we choose to adopt their perspective.... Second, the system of classification will not be based on present or past ideas about the etiology or cause of the attributes or acts to which deviance is imputed* unless those ideas be treated as meanings, rather than facts. . . . *(Freidson, 1970:224) (Emphasis added.)*

Freidson's point may be illustrated in the following way. Many authors attempt to distinguish physical conditions from social conditions. Certain conditions, such as floods, droughts, and earthquakes are perceived as acts of nature or aspects of the physical environment and therefore do not qualify as *social* problems. However, the characterization of a flood as physical or natural is part of our definition of the condition, not part of the condition. A flood is not a physical condition, but rather a condition that is defined as physical, rather than, for example, social or technological. Physical is a meaning that we attach to a condition, and as such, a meaning that might shift and change.

How might the meaning of a flood shift from that of a physical act of nature to something else? Recently the Mississippi River overflowed its banks, submerging and destroying a number of houses. The high water was the natural consequence of a late thaw and heavy rains, a condition that periodically affects this area. For this reason local zoning ordinances forbade the construction of permanent structures on this ground. Houses were, nevertheless, built on the land and stood immersed in water.

Investigation revealed that a contractor had bribed a city official in order to obtain building permits and had sold these houses to people from out of state who, unlike the local residents, had no knowledge of the effects of thaw and heavy rains in the area. Until the houses were built on the land, there had been no "flood," though the land had often been temporarily submerged. In what sense is the "flood problem" a consequence of the physical condition apart from the definition of the condition? Even the view that the causes of this minor disaster are natural, physical, or climatic is controversial and open to challenge, its rival being political corruption of the local officials and contractors.

A similar argument can be made in the case of the recent drought in the African Sehil region. The sources of the reduced rainfall have not been in dispute, except by a few persons who think atomic testing and pollution are responsible. The inability of the native population to survive in conditions of reduced rainfall has been laid to Western influences: encouragements to increase the population, and changes in the patterns of land use and harvesting. Without these, some argue, the native population would not have been so overextended that they could not survive a prolonged period of drought. Is this famine, therefore, a "natural" disaster?

A cautious and compromised view of the value-conflict approach argues that whether a condition is physical, genetic, physiological, psychological, medical, or technological, the process by which it becomes the focus of attention and defined as a social problem is *social*. We would go further and insist that the very characterization of a condition as physical, genetic, or physiological is *part of the definition of the condition* and not, analytically speaking, a characteristic of the objective condition itself. The nature and causes of a condition are negotiated through a fundamentally political process. It is not for sociologists of social problems to decide whether, for example, insanity is really an illness to which the medical model should be applied. They must, instead, study contentions of those who negotiate this definition, how they propose the mentally ill should be treated, the kind of personnel that should administer to them, or what agency should control the treatment process.

With this in mind, let us examine the typologies of social problems proposed by the value-conflict theorists. Fuller and Myers presented a threefold classification of physical, ameliorative, and moral problems. Their definitions of the three types of problems are:

> *The physical problem represents a condition which practically all people regard as a threat to their welfare, but value-judgments cannot be said to cause the condition itself.... The causation is thought of as nonhuman, resting outside the control of man. (1941a:27)*

> *Ameliorative problems represent conditions which people generally agree are undesirable in any instance, but they are unable to agree on programs for the amelioration of the condition.... The ameliorative*

problem is truly "social" in the sense that it is a man-made condition. By this we mean that value-judgments not only help to create the condition, but to prevent its solution. (1941a:28-9)

The moral problem represents a condition on which there is no unanimity of opinion throughout the society that the condition is undesirable in every instance. . . . Many people do not feel that anything should be done about it. . . . We have a basic and primary confusion in social values which goes much deeper than the questions of solution which trouble us in the ameliorative problem. (1941a:30)

The typology characterizes *conditions,* not definitions of conditions. Definitions enter the classification, but only in a minor role; the unanimity of disapproval distinguishes moral problems from physical and ameliorative problems. Presumably no one approves of floods or murder, but there are groups that defend child labor, a dissensus that distinguishes the moral problem from the other two categories. Having made a classification of conditions, the *causes of conditions* are elements of the typology. Value judgments cause ameliorative problems, but not physical problems, and moral problems are caused by conflicts and confusions in values. There is no doubt that Fuller and Myers refer to the condition itself, and not to its definition.

In the case of crime, certain moral judgments of our culture are to a large extent responsible for the criminal act *in the first place. (1941a:29) (Emphasis added.)*

The characterization of a condition as physical is part of its definition. In the same way, notions about the causes of a condition are also social constructions. In defining social problems, members of society construct theories about them and make causal inferences about conditions they find offensive, troublesome, or intolerable.

Given the thrust of their introductory statements, we might have expected Waller, Case, and Fuller and Myers to address the problem of how members determine and define the causes of such conditions. In the following quotation, Fuller and Myers begin such a discussion, but quickly turn from an analysis of how members construct causes to their (the sociologists') own analysis of the "real" causes of the condition. Not surprisingly, these "real" causes are social.

We find no public forums debating the question of what to do about preventing earthquakes and hurricanes: The causation is thought of as nonhuman, resting in natural forces outside the control of man. . . . If we may anticipate the time when scientists tell us how to prevent earthquakes, control hurricanes, and make rain for drought-stricken areas, we can imagine some elements of the population who will oppose the application of scientific techniques on the grounds that they are too costly and threaten budget balancing, or that they interfere with nature or God's will, or for some other reason. . . . At this point. . . we do have a man-made problem, since the will of certain groups is a causal element in the occurrence of the condition itself. (1941a:28-29) (Emphasis added.)

When Fuller and Myers indicate that the "causation is thought of as non-human," they carefully consider the members' constructions without making a commitment as to their accuracy. They discuss the common-sense causes that are part of the way people define the condition. However, they soon abandon what the members believe the causes of the condition to be (how those members define the condition) and proceed to discuss the "real man-made" causes of which members may or may not be aware. As they move from physical problems to ameliorative problems, the analysis of members' definitions of causation is entirely lost, and their discussion becomes an etiological consideration of crime, illegitimacy, and venereal disease. It becomes a discussion of conditions whose primary causes are value judgments or conflicts in values. This typology led Fuller and Myers back into an analysis of objective conditions strikingly similar to that of the functional approach of which they were so critical.

Waller's discussion contains the same subtle shift in emphasis. He says, "Social problems are conditions of which some of the causes *are felt to be human and moral."* (1936:925) (Emphasis added.) However, he also asserts that "the fact that a certain condition is, in some sense, humanly caused is an unrecognized, but essential criterion of the social problem." (1936:924) The former statement refers to the conceptions of the causes of conditions; the latter, however, deals with the actual causes of conditions, a quite different order of statement.

Another theme that preoccupied the value-conflict school led them even further from analysis of the definitional process and closer to the disorganization approach. They thought value judgments not only caused the condition and led people to define it as a problem, but also obstructed solutions to the problem and perpetuated it.

A value-scheme which prohibits frank discussion of sex problems in the home and school is a causal item in the existence of the condition, venereal disease. The same taboos which contribute to the causation of the condition frustrate public programs which are designed to eradicate it. Similarly, value-judgments which deny social acceptance to the mother of a child born out of wedlock, not only contribute causally to such conditions as abortions, infant mortality, and abandoned children, all of which are socially disapproved, but such value-judgments also obstruct efforts to solve the illegitimacy problem by impeding free discussion of it. (Fuller and Myers, 1941a:26)

This ironic and pessimistic theme is developed at great length in the value-conflict writings. It is likely that this was in reaction to functionalist-optimists who believed that social science and social engineering, given support from society, would help to solve social problems. The value-conflict writers not only considered social problems extremely intransigent and resistant to change, but contended that reformers themselves inhibit their solution. L. K. Frank patiently explained to an interplanetary visitor the difficulties of resolving the housing shortage:

We cannot just build houses, but must rely upon individual initiative and private enterprise to enter the field of building construction . . . we must use the price system to obtain the needed land which is someone's private property, to buy the necessary materials, and to hire the skilled labor . . . we must borrow capital on mortgages to finance these expenditures, paying a bonus to induce someone to lend that capital, and also pay interest on the loan, together with amortization quotas . . . then we must contrive to rent these dwellings in accordance with a multiplicity of rules and regulations about leases, and so on, . . . showing that to get houses built we must not infringe on anyone's rights of private property or freedom to make a profit. (1925:465-66)

This statement could have come from a social disorganization perspective, emphasizing as it does how some parts of a system inhibit the ability of other parts to realize system goals. Apart from his pessimism, Frank's position is indistinguishable from the social disorganization view.

The characteristic pessimism of value-conflict theorists regarding solutions to social problems extended to criticism and disdain for those attempting to solve social problems by tinkering with social institutions. Waller was particularly caustic about humanitarian reformers and social workers:

The humanitarian wishes to improve the condition of the poor, but not to interfere with private property. . . . He does not really want what he says he wants. . . . The urge to do something for others is not a very important determinant of change in our society, for any translation of humanitarianism into behavior is fenced in by restrictions which usually limit it to trivialities. (1936:28-30)

Waller singled out the social worker, whom he characterized as the professional humanitarian, though he considered these criticisms to be applicable to a good many sociologists as well:

The people who pay his salary and in countless ways assist him in his work of mercy are the persons who profit from the continuation of things as they are. . . . It is not ultimately the worst people, but the best people who blocked refor. . . . *The mental processes of social workers as a group may perhaps be described as aim-inhibited. . . . When one has accustomed himself to the thought that he can carry any proposed scheme only a certain distance, when one has formed the habit of breaking off any action, or speech, or thought, when it reaches a point where it may offend someone important, he loses the faculty of carrying mental processes through to completion. . . .*

Many sociologists are caught up in an almost identical situation, especially those who specialize in the study of social problems And such moral disunity effectively robs of significance the work of a great many brilliant men in our field. (1938:930-31)

These excerpts underline the irony that the very people who invoke their "humanitarian mores" to define conditions as social problems themselves subscribe to and support policies based on those same "mores" that insure the persistence of the condition. Setting aside the question of the validity of their observations, their judgments on the ineffectiveness of professionals as agents of social change deflected the value-conflict theorists from developing their initial focus on the definitional process, moving them back to the disorganization/dysfunction formulation. Not only has the analysis of the causes of objective conditions been reintroduced into the discussion, but a strong image has been drawn of a society unable to attain its goals, whose commitments in some sections prevent the realization of ends in others, whose members work at cross-purposes, not only with others, but with themselves. Social workers who try to relieve social problems contribute to them; humanitarian reformers profit from, and therefore, perpetuate the very conditions they crusade to remove. No better examples could be found to illustrate the concept of social disorganization.

RECENT VALUE-CONFLICT WRITINGS

In the preceding section we examined the "classic" writings of the value-conflict position. Although this position has been represented over the years in social problems textbooks, theoretical and empirical development of the formulation has not advanced beyond the early statements. More recently, there has been a renewed interest in the value-conflict perspective. A number of authors have refocused attention on the deficiencies of the functionalist formulation and have urged the adoption of an extension and amplification of a social definition approach. Some reflect a familiar mix in which a concern for the definitional process is undercut by the treatment of the objective conditions.

In *Social Problems: A Modern Approach* (1966), Howard S. Becker's introduction restated and updated Fuller and Myers' position. Sensitive to the ambiguous theoretical status of objective conditions, Becker presents a view that attempts to balance emphasis on the subjective element with an acknowledgment of the reality of objective conditions.

> *In short, as Fuller and Myers argued, no objective condition is necessarily a social problem. Social problems are what people think they are. But where does that leave the role of objective conditions? ... The question has two parts: Can people define any condition that exists as a social problem? Can people define a condition that does* not *exist— an illusion—as a social problem? (1966:5-6)*

Becker goes on to point out that people can define "nonexistent" conditions as social problems—witches, flying saucers—and then argues:

> *If any set of objective conditions, even nonexistent ones, can be defined as a social problem, it is clear that the conditions themselves do not either produce the problem, or constitute a necessary component of it. Why must we include them in our conception of social problems? We include them because the definition of most social problems refers to an area of social life that objectively and verifiably exists.*

> *Most citizens, and almost all social scientists in modern society feel the need to buttress their assertions about the existence of a social problem by referring to facts. They are aware that arguments which can be shown to have no factual foundation can be disposed of easily by opponents. (1966:6)*

Thus, even as Becker moves theoretically toward the assertion that objective conditions are neither necessary nor sufficient for the development of social problems, he tacitly retracts the assertion by conceptually making provision for such conditions. He provides explicitly for objective conditions on the basis of his "in most cases." A major consequence of this phrase is that the study of social problems focuses on "most of the cases," but leaves unsolved the theoretical significance of those other cases where objective conditions presumably do not exist. The balanced view suggests that definitions of social problems may be understood as reactions to conditions that "objectively and verifiably exist." Therefore the existence of the objective conditions helps explain the societal reaction to them. (For a systematic examination of the logical status of "objective conditions" as warrants for societal reactions, see Rains, 1975.)

This reduces the definition from a social construction of members of the society to a mere mechanical reaction to external events. The integrity of the definitional process is sacrificed for the balanced view.

Becker creates the same ambiguity that Fuller and Myers left in the wake of their reference to "the awareness of threat" in contrast to the "belief of threat." Do the conditions of social problems "objectively and verifiably exist"? Can the sociologist determine when there is no factual foundation for an argument? It is one thing to study the process of buttressing an argument and to observe how participants decide what the factual bases are, but quite another to stipulate that, apart from these definitional activities, the sociologist might or must make an independent assessment. For example, how could the sociologist decide that flying saucers *in fact* do not and never have existed? (Or witches, or extrasensory perception?) The sociologist of social problems could only examine how participants gather evidence and present claims about unidentified flying objects. The persistent effort to affirm the existence of objective conditions in social problems denies the significance *in their own right* of the conditions participants claim to exist, how participants interpret and evaluate those conditions, and how they organize their actions.

In a recent article, Blumer (1971) directly confronts the issue of the sociologist's primary concern with the objective conditions. Asserting that this concern "reflects a gross misunderstanding of the nature of social problems," he states:

Current sociological theory and knowledge, in themselves, just do not enable the detection or identification of social problems. Instead, sociologists discern social problems only after they are recognized as social problems by and in a society. Sociological recognition follows in the wake of societal recognition. . . .

If conventional sociological theory is so decisively incapable of detecting social problems and if sociologists make this detection by following and using the public recognition of social problems, it would seem logical that students of social problems ought to study the process by which a society comes to recognize its social problems. Sociologists have conspicuously failed to do this. (1971:299-300)

Blumer then presents a natural history that extends and makes the process of collective definition the focus of research and theory, arguing that:

Knowledge of the objective make-up of social problems is essentially useless because . . . social problems do not lie in the objective areas to which they point, but in the process of being seen and defined in the society." (1971:305-6)

Armand Mauss, author of a recent social problems text, aligns himself with the subjective approach, acknowledging his debt to the work of Becker and Blumer:

It is the position of this book that all social problems are produced by the behaviors of publics, interest groups, and/or pressure groups and that these are therefore very important social phenomena to understand. (1975:13)

Individuals and interest groups will simply generate social problems out of their own interests, with or without the data from objective reality. This is the theoretical point of view of what we might call "subjectivists" (to distinguish them from the "objectivists"). (1975:35)

However, Mauss then presents a formulation of "social *problems* as simply a kind of social *movement*" arguing that "the characteristics of social problems are typically also those of social movements." (1975:38) His interest in the definitional processes of social problems as such is narrowly confined to the argument that:

. . . social problems arise during these times of social change, not so much because of concomitant conditions like strain, disorganization, anomie, and the like, but simply because more people have more time, more resources, and more energy *to address social conditions, to define some of them as problematic and to engage in the processes of collective behavior which will produce social problem movements. (1975:44)*

The remainder of Mauss' theoretical chapter is an elaboration of Blumer's typology of social movements. The issue of the contingencies of social problems definition is abandoned in favor of topics such as the structural characteristics of social movements, recruitment and retention of members, leadership, and mobilization.

Two other articles extend the social definition approach. Hewitt and Hall (1973) treat the process through which members of a society construct causal explanations of a problematic situation. Ross and Staines (1972) explore the notion that the process of definition must be understood politically. The contrast between these two articles is instructive. The first, using an ethnomethodological perspective, consistently maintains the focus of attention on the members' conceptions and definitions of social reality. The second, drawing on the literature of political science, offers a number of valuable insights, but presents a conceptually mixed and uncertain focus on the members' definitional process.

Hewitt and Hall introduce the concept of "quasi-theories" ("ad hoc explanations brought to problematic situations to give them order and hope")

(1973:367) in order to discuss how members of a society talk about social problems, invent cures, and rationalize these cures with supportive causal analyses. Hewitt and Hall assert that when members of a society perceive a situation as problematic, they seek both explanations that will make it non-problematic and remedies to reestablish order and meaning.

> *The use of quasi-theories involves the postulation of a cure, followed by an analysis of cause and effect that supports the cure. . . .*
>
> *Once a cure has been announced, actors draw on the social stock of knowledge to construct an analysis of cause and effect that supports the cure. . . . The inference from cure to core problem is supported by a redefinition of other aspects of the problematic situation as essentially illusory. The causal analysis is extended by formulating causal generalizations. . . . Illustrations and examples are brought to bear which help establish the validity of the causal or explanatory scheme being used. . . . Support is sought in more general values, beliefs and social perspectives. . . .*
>
> *Once a given quasi-theory has been adopted, an endless store of ammunition can be mustered in its defense. (1973:370-372)*

They describe how members construct causal accounts of situations and propose to consider "the conditions under which solutions and explanations are generated and found convincing." (374) Significantly, they make no attempt to evaluate whether the members' accounts are, in fact, correct, for the correctness or accuracy of the causal account is not at all the issue. The members' causal account is one part of their effort to do something about a social problem. The relevant question is, "What makes such accounts convincing to members?"

In contrast, Ross and Staines' article (1972), which also deals with members' constructions of causal explanations, illustrates the ambiguities that have characterized the value-conflict position. They envision private interest groups recognizing a problem, public debate and social conflict concerning the problem, and a set of outcomes, legislation, or policy determining the final nature of the problem. One aspect of the public debate is the attribution of responsibility for the problem, either to "personal" or "system" factors. Some groups find it convenient to blame the system, others find it advantageous to blame the victims for their misfortunes.

Although Ross and Staines' discussion appears to parallel and complement Hewitt and Hall's focus on how members construct causal accounts to buttress their proposed cures, at several points they introduce the notion that these causal constructions may be viewed as either "true" or "false" in objective reality.

System blame is based on a recognition of structural and systemic inequities and weaknesses. *Many underdogs lack the political sophistication to make the attributional inference of system blame. That is,* since they fail to understand the system, *they are in a weak cognitive position to blame the system. Their more militant and sophisticated peers, however,* do have the ability to infer systemic weaknesses *and these systemic diagnoses may, over time, become consensual among underdogs. (1972:29) (Emphasis added.)*

In this passage, Ross and Staines go beyond a consideration of how members decide to blame the system or the victims. They indicate that those who blame the system are right and those who blame the victims are simply not sophisticated enough to understand the system is really to blame. The authors shift from studying how members attribute blame and engage in the attribution of blame from their own perspective. In doing so, they claim for themselves the abilities and sophistication that apparently all but the most militant underdogs lack. This confusion in their work is evident in the following passage:

The way in which interested parties handle the conflict over problem definition and related matters has important implications for policy outcomes. The accuracy *of problem diagnosis, for example, determines in part the effectiveness of policy decisions. Thus, if inordinate emphasis is* erroneously *assigned to personal factors in the diagnosis of a social problem—*a common mistake we suspect—*the resulting policies and programs will founder against situational or structural impediments which the diagnosis fails to acknowledge. (1972:36) (Emphasis added.)*

While Ross and Staines' emphasis on the political aspects of the collective definition process sharpens their appreciation of the members' point of view, like Merton, they maintain a position that endows the sociologist with superior knowledge and more analytic ability than those who are engaged in defining social problems. The notion that a diagnosis may be accurate or inaccurate introduces the perspective of the objective observer.

This reversion to the positivist concern for the "objective reality" is also characteristic of two other articles in which a critical posture toward the functionalist formulation is assumed only to propose "scientific standards" to define social problems. Manis offers a definition of social problems based on a critique of the disorganization approach. Emphasizing the subjective element in Merton's definition, he states, "Like other sociologists, Merton has deleted the objective criteria from his definition." (1974a:309) As a corrective, he proposes to develop wholly objective standards. Manis is impressed with the emerging norms and values of the scientific community and believes its knowledge and practices may be applied as a guide and model for the rest of society.

I propose the use of scientific knowledge and value as the basis for determining conditions harmful to the members of a society. . . . (1974b:3)

Determining whether given social phenomena are necessary or beneficial to human welfare, rather than unneeded or harmful, is desirable. (1974b:6)

. . . [Therefore] social problems are those social conditions identified by scientific inquiry and values as detrimental to the well-being of human societies. (1974a:314)

That one who offers such a definition should be critical of social disorganization or functional theory is puzzling. This point of view would seem to share the same burdens of specifying what the goals of human societies are, and providing methods for determining when a society is threatened or harmed by a given practice. Manis' optimism that "the scientific community" does and can in practice provide such a standard is not one that is universally shared, even among scientists. That question aside, it is not clear how the identification of conditions by those standards represents an advance over social disorganization theory.

Westhues is also critical of the functionalist perspective, but his own definition of social problems as "systemic costs" is barely distinguishable from it:

Problems are defined as costs of the particular form of socio-cultural organization a given society manifests. . . . Instead of defining as problems those phenomena which do not fit into or satisfy the given order, problems are defined as those qualities or aspects of the given order that do not satisfy some outside criterion. . . . The question raised in this approach is fundamentally, out of all possible gratifications, what does it cost members of a given society to be gratified according to the structure of their society? This approach calls into question society itself, and asks what one has to forego in order to live in it, and why. (1973:424)

Unfortunately, Westhues provides no clues as to how the outsider may construct the criteria for the cost-benefit analysis. As we have seen, this problem is characteristic of all approaches that are based on assessments of social conditions by "objective observers." Westhues' use of the concept "systemic costs" to replace terms favored by social disorganization theorists does nothing to resolve this problem.

Our brief survey of contemporary writings on social problems theory indicates that while all recent contributions take the functional paradigm to task, they offer a diversity of programs in its place. The most successful of these, we believe, is guided by the insights of ethnomethodology. (Hewitt and Hall, 1974) Blumer's work extends the line of thought of the value-conflict school, but does not focus on its logical difficulties. Ross and Staines attempt to graft the contributions of political science to the definitional process, but in so doing, further compound the confusion in the value-conflict literature on the issue of the importance of the subjective element in social problems. Finally, both Manis and Westhues, despite their critical posture, appear to restate the disorganization point of view, each using a slightly new metaphor.

4

Social Problems and Deviance: Some Parallels

In the preceding chapter, we examined the work of a series of writers who, over a period of fifty years, have attempted to reformulate the sociology of social problems. The central thrust of these attempts has been to shift the focus of analysis from the causes of objective social conditions to the processes by which members of a society define those conditions as problems. We have been struck by the fact that with the single exception of the ethnomethodologists Hewitt and Hall, sociologists have failed to develop a theoretical statement that is unencumbered by the conventional concern with the causes of objective conditions. Elements of the functional approach persist that create inconsistencies and contradictions in their formulations. Although most of these writers announce their break with the dominant social disorganization theory of social problems with dramatic statements in support of the definitional approach, they have been deflected from the logical thrust of this approach.

The reader may question why we give such close attention to writings that appear to be logically inconsistent and that contain conceptual anomalies. It is not our intent to pick through this literature in order to berate or bury the work of these writers. Indeed, we believe their work provided the base for a radically different perspective on the study of social problems. We believe it significant and worthy of genuine puzzlement that such a variety of writers over such along period of time should have written in the same vein, yet fail to realize their theoretical mission.

The efforts of the value-conflict theorists underline the apparent difficulty of constructing a theory that focuses on the social definitional process to the point of excluding consideration of the objective conditions. This difficulty may rest in part in the counter-intuitive nature of the argument itself—after all, the definitions must be about *something!*—but as we indicated in Chapter 1, the definitional processes are not impenetrable, inaccessible, or difficult to identify and describe. In this chapter we shall explore the idea that specific forms of membership or participation in society may account for the failure of these writers to maintain consistent attention on the definitional process.

In examining what we consider the puzzling pattern of unrealized value-conflict theory, it is helpful to consider other examples of the social definitional approach in sociology. In particular, the so-called "labeling theory of deviance," which Rubington and Weinberg (1971) identify as one of five approaches to the study of social problems, is instructive in clarifying the issues that deflect definitional approaches from their stated aims. We shall, therefore, briefly characterize the parallels between the development of value-conflict and labeling theories and the similar difficulties they have encountered.

LABELING THEORY

The labeling theory of deviance has been the standard-bearer of the social definitional approach in sociology generally, and it has borne the brunt of the criticism of this form of theorizing. Although it is a relatively recent development compared to the value-conflict theory, it has generated a much more extensive literature. Labeling theory and its empirical research are a center of controversy among criminologists and other students of deviance. This controversy has spilled over into discussions of the sociology of social problems—so much so that the writings of Fuller and Myers are often called "the labeling theory of social problems."

Labeling theory has been subject to the same problems of logical development that have plagued value-conflict and other subjectivist approaches to social phenomena. By linking our discussion of the value-conflict writings to those of labeling theory, we emphasize that the problems examined in the preceding chapter are not simply errors or shortcomings of the various writers who have contributed to that literature. The parallels in the development of these two theories may suggest a solution to the puzzle of why they have come to share a common theoretical impasse.

In particular, we note three striking similarities in the two theoretical perspectives: (1) social problems and deviance are conceived as products of social processes in which members of a group, community, or society perceive, interpret, evaluate, and treat behaviors, persons, and conditions as problems; (2) they shift attention away from the behaviors and conditons of those who are commonly thought to constitute the problem back to members of the society who conceive those behaviors and conditions as problems; (3) such a focus demands a theory and method to document and account for the symbolic processes through which the meanings of such behaviors and conditions are generated and institutionalized.

Like the value-conflict theory, labeling theory was shaped by an explicit criticism and rejection of previous formulations. It rejected the notion that acts could be identified as deviant with reference to norms or values independent of how members of the society recognize and treat such behaviors. Labeling theorists argued further that explanations of deviance could not be conceptualized as characteristics of individuals—whether they be cultural, psychological, economic, political, or genetic—but must be sought in the interactive process between those who create and apply rules and those they single out as deviant. Labeling theory rejected the dominant etiological approach that sought to differentiate between those who commit deviant acts and those who do not. It abandoned the notion that any individual characteristics could account for the differentiation of deviants from nondeviants. Statements of labeling formulation, however, failed to shed completely the burdens of conventional etiology, and subsequent criticsm and controversy has focused on ambiguities that reflect the failure to press the distinctive insights of the labeling perspective to their logical conclusions.

Although Tannenbaum (1938) discussed the concept of *tagging*, Lemert's *Social Pathology*, published in 1951, is most commonly acknowledged as the first statement of the labeling point of view. Lemert emphasized the process of societal reaction as the basis for the definition and differentiation of deviance and argued that the origins of deviant behavior are so idiosyncratic and situationally variable that they defy scientific study or generalization.

This shift in focus from the presumed deviant and deviant acts to the definitional activities of others was blurred in Lemert's discussion as well as in Becker's statement (1963) of the perspective ten years later. While both of these writers made clear their intent to develop an alternative to the conventional formulation, their statements have been interpreted by proponents and critics alike to contain conflicting and contradictory meaning, so much so that the development of labeling theory has been impeded by interminable textual analysis.

The sources of this confusion may be found in key passages in Lemert's and Becker's writings. In preparing the ground for his theory of *sociopathic behavior,* Lemert postulated "modalities of behavior and deviations from those modalities." (1951b:22) He further posited societal reactions to such deviations, i.e., that such deviations are defined and treated as deviant by members of the society. Having postulated deviations from modalities of behavior as the basis for societal reactions, Lemert was committed to the theoretical position that these reactions were reactions to *something,* that is, to empirically observable behaviors.

This commitment, reflected in Lemert's discussion of the social and cultural sources of deviation and differentiation, is generally unrecognized by critics as well as those who support his work. In his discussion of the postulates, Lemert moves from (1) a statistical conception of deviation ("deviations from modalities") to (2) a conception of normative deviation ("differentiation which can be related to modal structures and values") to (3) a "narrower sociological viewpoint" in which "deviations are not significant until they are organized subjectively and transformed into active roles and become social criteria for assigning status." (1951b:75) This last conception is the basis for Lemert's oft-cited distinction between primary and secondary deviation that is central to his theory of sociopathic behavior. Primary deviation refers to initial acts of deviation committed by persons which they may ignore, rationalize, or disavow, so that such acts are not systematically integrated into their self-conceptions. Lemert conceived of secondary deviations as expressions of behavioral systems organized by the person's "defense, attack, or adjustment to the overt and covert problems created by the consequent societal reactions" to his or her primary deviations. (1951b:76)

The societal reaction perspective as originally articulated contained a theoretical compromise. It presupposed an objective act, observable and definable by the sociologist using statistical standards of normality, and it assumed normative standards are an essential feature of social systems. Societal reactions were conceived of as reactions to acts that violated social norms presumed to exist in the society. Norms, then, provided the sociologist with a vantage point from which to define, observe, and classify behaviors as deviant.

Becker provided for an objectively observable basis for the classification of behavior. The two axes of his typology represent both the perspective of members ("perceived as deviant/not perceived as deviant") and that of the independent observer ("rule-breaking/obedient behavior"). Like Lemert, Becker focused on the object being defined, i.e., the behavior of the individual, as the stimulus for the application of labels. Four of the five empirical chapters of *Outsiders* report not how groups create deviance by producing rules and applying them to others, but rather how persons come to participate in the kinds of actions that others find offensive. Similarly, while Lemert has insisted that sociologists study secondary deviation, much of his own work (on check forgers and paranoia, for example) deals with primary deviation. These remnants of conventional etiological analysis have invited the interpretation that labeling theory attempts to explain not deviant acts, but deviant identities, behavior systems, life-styles, and subcultures. Rains has elegantly summarized the dilemma:

> It is not possible to speak about the relationship between deviance and social control without deciding how to speak about what "reactions to deviance" are reactions to. It is not simply a practical matter to be settled so as to get on with the analysis, for a clear decision on this deceptively ordinary matter both expresses and generates theoretical commitments which the analysis must then serve. A decision about what 'reactions to deviance' are reactions to tends also to become a statement about the degree to which such reactions are warranted, and this more implicit matter of moral tone has also plagued labeling theorists and their critics. (1975:2)

The theoretical impasse that Lemert and Becker have created for the labeling theory of deviance underlines the pervasive influence of the conventional concerns in this field of specialization. Sociologists, like ordinary members of the society, seem intent on asking, "What makes people commit deviant acts?"

even when their theory poses a prior question, "How do people come to define such acts as deviant?" Labeling theory deflected criticism of the "subjectivism" of an uncompromising definitional formulation by turning attention back to the etiological question.

We view the return to etiological questions as reasonable accommodation that acknowledges the importance of objective as well as subjective aspects of deviance and social problems. Lemert balanced the concept of social differentiation with that of secondary deviation, complementing societal reaction processes with the concern for the development of sociopathic behavior. Becker's discussion of rule making is followed by chapters on rule breakers, just as Fuller and Myers qualified their definition with the statement "the objective condition is necessary, but not in itself sufficient to constitute a social problem." For all of their efforts to achieve a balanced theoretical stance, the accommodation has been rejected by the editors of the leading text on deviance and social problems, who characterize the labeling and value-conflict formulations as "heedless subjectivism." (Merton and Nisbet, 1971:806)

INTERPRETATION

We have analyzed parallel problems of logical development in two related bodies of writings. It is puzzling that the definitional approaches to deviance and social problems should be so difficult to maintain as a consistent sociological argument. We suggest that this difficulty is related to the ways sociologists participate in different social groups. In particular, we shall discuss three kinds of membership: sociologists as ordinary members of society, as members of a profession, and as participants in the definitional process itself.

Sociologists as Ordinary Members

Sociologists who study their own society are, of course, also members of it. As members they have their own views of what social conditions exist and which ones are problems. We do not deny the possibility that sociologists may, on the basis of their own values and moral judgments, identify and define certain conditions as social problems. But this practice must be clearly separated from a *theoretical* mandate to do so.

In recognition of this membership based source of definitions, sociologists have two methodological options. One is to suspend their own definitions as external to the phenomena under investigation and attend solely to the definitions of members. No question would ever arise concerning divergences between the sociologists' and the members' definitions or perspective. The second option is that sociologists treat their own definitional activity as part of the phenomenon. This behavior might lead sociologists to examine the grounds on which they define a given condition as a problem. On what grounds do conditions command their attention? What common-sense constructions do they use to attribute meanings? Both options suggest a kind of reflexive examination usually absent from writings on social problems. Unfortunately, neither is easily translated into a set of procedures guaranteeing that attitudes, values, and opinions sociologists hold by virtue of their membership in society (or a sector of class of a society) will not influence their professional thinking or research.

Sociologists as Members of a Profession

A second type of pressure away from analysis of definitional questions stems from the fact that sociology competes with a variety of other disciplines and professions.

Ideas about causation are basic to how the work of the scientific community is organized. The division of work into specialties or disciplines, including the departmental structure in universities, reflects these ideas about where different parts of the world fit in the overall body of scientific knowledge. Some phenomena are the exclusive property of one discipline. Others are considered multidimensional, with complex causal structure, and may be claimed by more than one discipline or by an interdisciplinary program. Those who presume to research a problem outside of their discipline may be accused of reductionism, suggesting a disrespect for the nature of the phenomenon, or of dilettantism.

When sociologists study the development and organization of professions, they usually view the causal analyses of various disciplines as expressions of professional ideologies. Similarly, they typically see causal analyses of citizen groups or moral crusaders as rhetoric or simply the opinion or sentiment of some segments of the population. That is, when sociologists treat causal assertions made by other groups, they examine them as expressions of perspectives that reflect the assumptions, values, and interests of those groups rather than objective statements about reality. This practiced skepticism, however, is not applied to the sociologists' own causal analyses or explanations of social phenomena. Yet, on what grounds do the causal analyses of the sociologist differ from those of other groups in society? On what basis, for example, did Fuller and Myers dismiss members' definitions of floods as natural disasters as less real than their own view of the man-made causes of that condition? On what basis did Ross and Staines conclude that "the system" causes poverty rather than that the victims are themselves to blame?

The research perspective that seeks to decide which causal explanation is the most valid diverts attention for the question posed by the social definitional approach. The question is not which explanation is more accurate, true, or even elegant, but rather how is it decided which will be accepted in a competition or conflict among them? The commonplace view that scientific inquiry may determine the causes of a phenomenon and provide the basis for adjudicating the validity of competing causal statements ignores the fact that such statements are the *social constructions of social scientists*. As such, they must be treated as objects to be explained, and the form and content of those constructions must be taken as problematic. If, for example, the preponderance of research indicates that homosexuality is a disease and not a life-style, this may only indicate that the psychiatric medical establishment is more powerful, prestigious, and in favor with institutions granting research funds than social science disciplines. If the fortunes of academic disciplines rise and fall with reference to funding policies, the relative development of research findings among the different disciplines provides no basis for conclusions about the true causes of homosexuality or any other phenomenon.

If we alter our frame of reference so that the causal statements of sociologists and other scientists are part of the data for our analysis, we may ask what distinctive role they play in the process through which social problems are defined. Then competing causal analyses may be viewed as the ideologies of professions that have adopted the language of science as a strategy to promote their professional interests. This reminds us that the founding fathers of the social sciences were outspoken reformers; they established social science departments in universities as part of their programs of reform. Establishing a place in the university gave them prestige and a base of operations for their efforts in social reform. As Hughes points out, the same may be said of occupations that attempt to attain professional status:

> *As an occupation strives for professional standing it generally seeks and may get a place in the institutions called universities. It will usually claim that the work of the profession rests upon a discipline, perhaps upon a science. . . .*
>
> *I want to emphasize that the departments of social science are as much historic institutions as logical divisions. Each one is the product either of social movements inside the academic world, or of movements outside which later got into the academic world. (1971:410, 503)*

This conception of academic disciplines provides a new perspective on social science theories. By viewing sociology, psychology, social psychiatry, economics, and social work as ambitious social movements, disciplines, or professions, we may apply to them and their knowledge the same tools we bring to bear on the activities of any social group. Statements about causation, levels of analysis, or the nature of a phenomenon are efforts to stake claims to certain subject matter.

When the resources for which various disciplines compete are scarce, theories may be advanced to lay exclusive claim to specific areas of research or to maintain control of the existing organization of academic specialization.

Competition for academic domains and institutional resources may take place in curriculum committees within universities. For example, such a committee may be presented with a proposal from the history department to add a course in Urban History. The department of sociology, which regularly offers Urban Sociology in its program, may object to history's proposal, questioning its theoretical basis, the empirical materials and literature to be covered, and the instructor's qualifications. The competition between academic units frequently develops into open conflict when one department proposes to appoint a scholar trained in its discipline, but whose research and writing has strayed into another department's disciplinary territory. In such situations, departments may claim the right to approve or veto each other's appointments.

Just as departments may attempt to gain exclusive control in conflicts with other disciplines, they may also form alliances within the university for the same purpose. These may be called interdisciplinary programs, area studies, or committees. The organizational rationales for such developments usually argue that the subject matter in question is so complex as to require multiple disciplinary perspectives and skills. Such proclamations may simply reflect the inability of any single department to gain exclusive control over an area of study. In some instances, a given discipline may be so prestigious and academically powerful that it is necessary for less prestigious disciplines to establish alliances in order to invade a field of research. Thus, social scientists may assemble a multidisciplinary team in making proposals for research grants in a closely guarded field like medicine. Hughes says of such interdisciplinary arrangements:

> Interdisciplinary work implies that each party to it means to respect the other's boundaries, while seeing to it that his own discipline gets its share of money, attention and space in publications. Interdisciplinary work generally means that the parties are determined not to merge their disciplines . . . that there is resistance to reorganization of the university and of research bodies in a way to correspond to the present and emergent state of the frontiers of knowledge. I mean to suggest that the organization of the university by disciplines should itself be a matter of study, something on which we keep an open mind. (1971:410)

Although this view of social science theory may seem overly cynical, it enables us to place these activities within our analysis of how sociologists' definitions and explanations of social conditions lead them away from maintaining a theoretically consistent approach to social problems. Just as subjects studied by sociologists seldom view themselves as they are viewed by researchers, it is not surprising that sociologists do not subject their own activities to detached observation and analysis. However, their statements about causation of social phenomena, their attitudes toward interdisciplinary research, and their defense of the logic of the organization of disciplines within the university cannot be understood as a reflection of an empirical reality external to and independent of the statements made about them. Psychology and sociology departments, for example, do not exist in universities because there really are different kinds or levels of phenomena in objective reality. They exist because different groups have been able to convince administrators that they deserve the same treatment and dignity accorded existing units within the university.

If we discover that a given topic is treated in one department rather than in another, this tells us little about the subject itself but much about who has been able to claim custody of it. These claims are consequential for the kind of social problems definitions they produce. Homosexuality is one thing when it is taught as a topic in abnormal psychology and quite another when it is taught in a course on counter-cultural life-styles or as a topic in the modern family. These features of the organization of academic disciplines lead us to view scientific facts and knowledge about social conditions as products of that organization, not as reflections of the phenomena they purport to describe and explain.

Sociologists as Participants in Social Problems

Not only are sociologists members of a discipline that acts to promote its interests within the university, they are also members of a profession that participates in social problems activities in the wider world. They may press the sociological perspective in competition for research grants and lobby for representation on foundation and governmental research review committees. When funds become available in heretofore unsupported research areas, sociologists may reorient their research programs to fit the specifications and goals of the new funding policies. On this point Cressey observed:

> *Perhaps social phenomena are extensively perceived as social problems only when some proposal for eradication (or at least, change) is well publicized and well financed. Thus, "mental health" seems to have become a major social problem only after the National Institute of Mental Health was established to improve the nation's mental health. Somewhat as a consequence of the fact that mental health was established as a social problem in this way, social scientists discovered that they are experts on mental health problems. By the same token, creation of the new cabinet post, Secretary of Transportation, probably means that "transportation" soon will become a major social problem and that increasing numbers of social scientists will discover that they are experts on transportation problems. (1967:107)*

There is little doubt that the National Institutes of Health and of Mental Health have given impetus and incentive to the sociological profession to develop and extend its disciplinary domain into various new areas. In such lobbying activities, sociological theories are consequential for the ways such problems as mental illness, child abuse, and mental retardation are defined and explained. We note again the importance of distinguishing the extension and growth of sociological theorizing and research about specific social phenomena from any conclusions about the "truth" of the knowledge.

Let us examine a case of interprofessional competition in which the sociological profession moved from a position of, perhaps, bemused spectatorship to that of active participation in the definition of mental disorders. For many years psychiatrists and clinical psychologists have argued over the medical nature of mental disturbances. Beginning in the mid-1950's, their professional organizations convened committees and panels and issued reports on whether clinical psychologists, who lack medical training, should be licensed to dispense therapy to patients or clients with mental disorders. Many issues emerged in these discussions. Psychiatrists argued that mental disorders were diseases, and only a physician could treat them. Psychologists attached the abstract theory of illness and pointed to their own extensive studies of abnormal psychology. Psychiatrists emphasized the prominence of drug therapy in current treatment of mental disorders and asked how the nonmedical psychologist could direct such treatment. Fee schedules were also at issue: would third parties, such as insurance companies, pay psychologists the same fees as they would psychiatrists? Indeed, were psychologists qualified for *any* reimbursement for services rendered to those suffering mental disorders?

At one point in the interchange the psychiatrists confronted the psychologists with the fact that the psychological profession had little control over one of its categories of clinicians—social psychologists. They noted that a large number of sociologists also use this term to refer to themselves, and this, they claimed, would confuse the public. The psychiatrists argued that the psychological profession had insufficient control over the certification of social psychologists to warrant granting them license to engage in the treatment of mental disorders. The American Psychological Association, therefore, asked if the American Sociological Association would consider forbidding its members to use the term "social psychologist." The sociologists declined. Had the psychiatrists challenged sociologists more directly about their competence, say, to act as consultants to agencies concerned with juvenile delinquency, there is no doubt that sociologists would have responded with vigor. (Goode, 1960)

These interprofessional conflicts which appear to be scientific debates about rival theories, research findings, and causal explanations are data par excellence for the study of the definitional process. They may be viewed as conflicts between the definitions of a social problem sponsored by two professional associations, a conflict that a sociologist might investigate and analyze without subscribing to any definition of what mental disorders really are. The sociologist would examine the statements and counterstatements as part of the process of defining mental illness.

Given this view of professional and interdisciplinary disputes and competition, is there less reason to suspect that the activities of sociologists are expressions of hidden agendas and interests than those of psychiatrists or clinical psychologists? After all, if as Fuller and Myers argued, the *real* causes of venereal diseases are social, does this not suggest that sociologists should run the venereal disease bureaucracy? Should not the research grants and training programs go to departments of sociology rather than to medical schools? Perhaps those who staff these programs and bureaucracies should be required to complete an approved course of study in sociology.

We need not impute venality or Machiavellian motives to Fuller and Myers. On the other hand, it would be naive and ethnocentric to deny that their statements (and those of many other sociologists) do not have consequences for professional sociology. We do not mean to imply that sociologists should not engage in research to document social conditions. We simply make the point that various groups find it to their advantage to promote and call attention to some antecedents of any condition and to ignore or dismiss others as insignificant.

The logic of the value-conflict approach would insist that when persons, professions, or organizations, press for public recognition of their theory or explanation of some condition, they cease to analyze the social problem and become a part of it. Willard Waller recognized this problem forty years ago and recommended:

> *When our attitude toward a phenomenon is involved in our concept of it, logical difficulties arise which can only be avoided by shifting to an inclusive point of view which enables us to study both the thing and our attitude toward it. (1936:922)*

Sociologists have sometimes been aware of this dilemma, but their response has been to shift to an inclusive point of view that defines their own role, not as one category of member among many, but rather as scientists who are laboring on behalf of society, protecting society, trying to improve society, and providing expertise to determine the most effective policy. (See Merton and Nisbet, 1971: Chapter 1.) They invariably fail to consider the sociologist as an interested party to social problems definitions—as empire builders, academic entrepreneurs, lobbyists, and expert consultants. In short, they fail to subject their own activities to the kind of political analysis they would apply to all other categories of participants in the definitional process.

When the sociologist has a different view of the world from some other group or organization, such differences are not treated as member-member conflicts, but rather, for example, as manifest versus latent problems. The technical quality of the language shields the sociologist from serious scrutiny. This tactic is not confined to the functionalist theorists from whom it certainly might be expected. Fuller and Myers and Waller do not hesitate to treat the causes claimed by others as part of the definition while viewing their own causal statements as part of the analysis. Similarly, in his section "What Can Social Science Contribute?" Becker (1966:23-28) casts the sociologist in the helping role of expert, supplying knowledge, falsifying incorrect assumptions, and otherwise assisting in developing rational, informed policies. More recently, Manis (1974a,b), in a statement that is critical of Merton's concept of latent social problems, himself invokes the mantle of science to exempt his own definitions as data for an understanding of how social problems emerge and develop.

The definitional approach, then, pursued to its logical conclusion, requires that the sociologist, as a participant in the politics of defining social problems, be denied the special status of one who stands outside the process as objective observer or scientist. *Whether the sociologist will be treated as a scientist by other participants in the process and accorded the special status of a disinterested and unbiased expert is a problematic, empirical question.*

Let us consider two schematic, but not so hypothetical situations to illustrate this question:

Case 1: The president of a university, trained as a psychologist, publicly states that women will continue to occupy inferior positions within university faculties in terms of rank, salary, and tenure because they lack the required skills and motivations to succeed because of early childhood training. These patterns of differential achievement by sex are observable from the age of two. No amount of ideological rhetoric can get around this fact.

Case 2: In a debate on a bill to legalize sexual acts between consenting adults of the same sex, a legislator says she will vote against the bill because she fears for the safety of young children.

Confronted with these statements, sociologists are likely to ask whether or not the assertions made are factually true and whether inferences based on them are logically warranted. Addressing the statements in this way, sociologists may find it difficult to remain aloof and uninvolved. With reference to Case 1, sociologists might argue that discrimination on tenure committees, rather than early socialization, explains observed differences in the position of women faculty members. In Case 2, sociologists might refute the stereotype that most homosexuals are also child molesters. By responding in this manner to the assertions of community members about social conditions, the sociologists are no longer simply analysts of social problems, but participants in the process of definition that should be the subject matter of study.

The hypothetical cases poses quite different questions for our approach to social problems—questions that do not address the truth of the assertions made by the participants. Quite apart from the validity of the statements made by the university president and the legislator, can such assertions about the status of women and homosexuals be sustained politically? Can they "get away with" making such statements? Who are the audiences to whom they are directed, and how will they respond? What other groups might appear to take issue with them? How strongly will these spokesmen defend their views? Whom would they cite or consult to document their assertions? If sociologists and psychologists are consulted and thus enter the controversy, what is the relative prestige of these two disciplines should they disagree? What body would have standing to refute their testimony or resolve their disagreement? All of these questions are logically independent of and unrelated to the question of the truth or falsity of the assertions.

To enter the policy-making process of social problems activities is to become subject to pressures that may lead to the abandonment of definitional questions in favor of the applied, practical, policy-oriented issues that are adjudicated by participants. For example, a sociologist may have researched the history of how marijuana came to be defined as an illegal drug. When called to testify as an expert, she is asked whether marijuana is, *in fact,* harmful to those who use it. If she is unwilling to address that issue, her expert status, whether coveted or not, will be short-lived. A partisan and personal view of the matter may lead her to respond to the question and claim expertise where there is none. For example, knowledge of how marijuana use was made a criminal offense provides no basis for testifying to its harmful psychological, physiological, or genetic effects. Similarly, an "expert" on social definitions of homosexuality who is testifying before a parliamentary committee is not asked how the phenomenon is defined, but whether or not homosexuals are also, *in fact,* dangerous child molesters. Thus, the very phrasing of the questions, as well as the responses of the "sociologist-expert" are data for the study of social problems.

Three kinds of pressures have been outlined that tend to deflect the attention of labeling and social problems theorists away from their chosen subject matter. As members of society they fail to examine their own interpretive activities. As members of an aspiring profession in a competitive organizational environment, vested interests make them compete in traditionally defined arenas. Finally, as individual experts they are expected to address practical policy questions and thus accept their underlying positivistic assumptions.

CONCLUSION

Our examination of the difficulties that have attended the efforts of value-conflict theorists to produce a formulation faithful to their radical conception of social problems leads us to the view that a sociology of social problems must take the members' perspective as the starting point, focusing in particular on definitional claims-making activities as the primary subject matter. Rather than investigate how institutional arrangements produce certain social conditions, we examine how individuals and groups become engaged in collective activities that recognize putative conditions as problems, and attempt to establish institutional arrangements.

We propose as the central interest of sociologists of social problems and deviance the interaction between claims-making groups and others regarding the definition of social conditions and what should be done about them. In contention throughout the social problems-producing process (as in the deviance-producing process) are the definitions of reality that groups and organizations assert, sponsor, impose, reject, or subvert. The initial definition of social reality may undergo modification and changes such that the condition asserted to be the problem at one point in time turns out to be a different and apparently unrelated condition at another point.

A central task of a theory of social problems and deviance is to describe and explain the definitional process in which morally objectionable conditions or behaviors are asserted to exist and the collective activities that become organized around *those assertions*. Such a theory would seek to explain how those definitions and assertions are made, the processes by which they are acted upon by institutions, and how those institutional responses do or do not produce socially legitimated categories of social problems and deviance.

If the subject matter is definitions of social problems, then *it is definitions that are socially processed*. In this sense, we can say that definitions have careers, one aspect of which is their institutionalization as official categories. In like manner, central to the subject matter of the sociology of deviance is the processing of the definitions of deviance which may result in the development of informally recognized and enforced categories, as well as the establishment of official categories and populations of deviants. The theoretical problem is to account for how categories of social problems and deviance are produced, and how methods of social control and treatment are institutionally established.

5

Social Problems as Claims-Making Activities

We have discussed the dominant approach to social problems and the dissent from the formulation developed from it. In this chapter we begin to systematically outline our own approach and discuss some of the issues it poses for the study of social problems. Our point of view is in part a reaction to the functional theory of social problems, as well as an extension and elaboration of the value-conflict writings. We intend to avoid the pitfalls that have drawn writers back to more traditional concerns; we wish to elaborate a conception of social problems that follows a social definition approach to its logical conclusion. Our effort may be viewed by some as a *reductio ad absurdum,* a one-sided statement about social phenomena that ignores or seems incompatible with other scientific realities. We hope that other readers find in our discussion a clearer demonstration of the kind of analysis that a number of writers have been attempting to fashion in the field of deviance and social problems for several decades. Our statement, then, is an attempt to explain and explore a type of argument, and to describe just what kind of formulation is suggested by the statement that "social problems are what people think they are."

Our first task is to discover a subject matter. In the past, the term *social problem* was perceived as the subject matter for the study of social pathology, disorganization, deviant behavior, value conflicts, and labeling. (Rubington and Weinberg, 1971) The designation of social problem as an indication of social pathology, or vice versa, simply applies two terms to the same subject matter. If prostitution, for example, is classified as a social pathology and also considered a social problem, the application of the second term in no way contributes to our understanding of prostitution. Is there a distinctive subject matter for the study of social problems?

The notion that social problems are a kind of *condition* must be abandoned in favor of a conception of them as a kind of *activity*. We call this *claims-making activity* and will offer a relatively formal definition of the phenomenon. We then examine attempts to explain social problems activities, particularly Fuller and Myers' formulation that "value judgments lead people to define conditions as social problems."

Fuller and Myers' concern with the determinants of definitions is premature and focuses attention away from a consideration of the phenomenon itself. Also, the use of values to explain social behavior is subject to a number of logical problems that lead us to abandon this type of theory.

Values, however, are an important element in social problems activities. In rejecting the notion that values may "cause" people to define conditions as problems, we argue that the *imputation* of values and interests may explain or provide accounts of activities to the participants, but they cannot provide explanations for the sociologist. Imputations of values and interests to the actions of others by participants in claims-making activities (as well as to their own actions) are *part* of the value-judgmental process and thus part of the data to be explained. We view values as linguistic devices that participants use to articulate their claims, or to persuade others to legitimize them.

SOCIAL PROBLEMS AS ACTIVITIES

Fuller and Myers defined a social problem as "a condition which is defined by a considerable number of persons as a deviation from some norm, which they cherish." (1941b:320) We have discussed the methodological problems inherent in referring to numbers of people in the definition of social problems. How many people? What must they do in order for the sociologist to place the condition in the social problems category and begin the analysis? These questions are insoluble. If we remove the reference to numbers of people, what do we have left? What kinds of conditions are social problems?

Our view is that any definition of social problems that begins "social problems are those conditions. . ." will lead to a conceptual and methodological impass that will frustrate attempts to build a specialized area of study. The question, then, is: if social problems cannot be conditions, what are they? Most succinctly, they are the activities of those who assert the existence of conditions and define them as problems.

It is helpful in developing a model for defining the subject matter for the study of social problems to refer to the study of occupations. This model is profitable for several reasons. The study of work and occupations is an area that is not beset with the terminological and definitional dilemmas that characterize the field of social problems. If we learn how that field manages to avoid these issues, perhaps we can construct a similar definition to structure the study of social problems.

While diverse theoretical views are represented in the study of occupations, the underlying sociological theory that guides our approach to social problems has also guided a major orientation of research on occupations, symbolic interactionism. The interactionist view in the sociology of occupations is evident in the writings of Hughes (1971) and his followers.

This body of literature may provide us with theoretical analogues for our study of social problems. The study of work and occupations is relevant in another way: social problems activities are the *work* of many people— journalists, doctors, politicians, social workers, consumer advocates, and union organizers. Many aspects of social problems may be approached through the study of the people who work in various stages of the process of creating social problems.

Our inquiry stands to profit from a convergence, or at least a compatibility, with the study of work and occupations which focuses on the activities by which men and women earn their livelihood. Whenever and wherever people are engaged in such activity, they provide the subject matter for the sociology of work. It does not matter whether only a few or a great many people are engaged in that activity. Conceptually, they are considered participants in the category "work." If very few practice the activity, we might observe, interview, and study them all. If a great number engage in the activity, we must find some means of drawing a sample. Even if only one person earns her livelihood at an activity, it is still possible to make it the subject of an occupational study—describing the activity, how she came to do the work, with whom she associates in performing her tasks, how her activities are affected by the presence or absence of co-workers or colleagues, and so on.

We want to define the subject matter of the sociology of social problems so that a researcher may carry through the analysis with the same reasonable procedure as the student of work and occupations. Just as the study of occupations examines how people earn their living, the study of social problems must look at how people define social problems. If a sociologist of occupations studying prostitution would look for people earning their livings at it, the sociologist of social problems would look for people engaged in defining (or promoting) the prostitution problem. The student of occupations sets out to describe work activity, elaborating its various forms and organization, and inventing concepts to make sense of and explain its variations. In the same way, the student of social problems should discover the nature of social problem activities and develop concepts that will most clearly and succinctly account for their special character. In each case, a distinctive kind of activity is singled out for attention: in the former case, the technical term for the activity is *work*. In the latter case, we must propose, define, and elaborate the technical term which we call claims-making activity.

A DEFINITION OF SOCIAL PROBLEMS

Our definition of social problems focuses on the process by which members of a society define a putative condition as a social problem. Thus, we define social problems as *the activities of individuals or groups making assertions of grievances and claims with respect to some putative conditions*. The emergence of a social problem is contingent upon the organization of activities asserting the need for eradicating, ameliorating, or otherwise changing some condition. *The central problem for a theory of social problems is to account for the emergence, nature, and maintenance of claims-making and responding activities.* Such a theory should address the activities of any group making claims on others for ameliorative action, material remuneration, alleviation of social, political, legal, or economic disadvantage.

Let us comment briefly on the word *putative* in the above definition. The dictionary defines this word as "reputed, hypothesized, or inferred." We use the word to emphasize that any given claim or complaint is about a condition *alleged* to exist, rather than about a condition whose existence we, as sociologists, are willing to verify or certify. That is, in focusing attention on the claims-making process, we set aside the question of whether those claims are true or false.

In an analysis of the logic of this position in the related area of the sociology of deviance, Rains states:

> *Like the term "alleged," "putative" is intentionally, even ostentatiously, careful talk, allowing one to speak of something without commitment to its actuality. As a way of handling the problem of how to speak about what "reactions to deviance" are reactions to, words like "putative" have similarly, if more pertinently served to beg the question. The phrase "reactions that impute mental illness" does not, after all, require mental illness in the same way that the phrase "reactions to mental illness" does. But just as "putative father" is an ambiguous term that may express several possible degrees of belief in a girl's claim, "putative deviation" permits a variety of not necessarily explicit theoretical stances toward the relationship between deviance and the societal reactions which impute it. (1975:3)*

We are interested in constructing a theory of claims-making activities, not a theory of conditions. Thus, the significance of objective conditions for us is *the assertions made about them,* not the validity of those assertions as judged from some independent standpoint, as for example, that of a scientist. To guard against the tendency to slip back into an analysis of the condition, we assert that even the existence of the condition itself is irrelevant to and outside of our analysis. We are not concerned whether or not the imputed condition exists. If the alleged condition were a complete hoax— a fabrication—we would maintain a noncommittal stance toward it unless those to whom the claim were addressed initiated their own analysis and uncovered it as a hoax.

Having stated the matter in the most extreme, and seemingly unreasonable, fashion, let us try to make it appear more sensible. Some objection to this position may stem from the fact that certain conditions do exist in the real world—out there. Objections may also be based on the view that some putative conditions appear to be just the phenomena that sociologists are trained to discover and verify. Let us discuss the second point first.

Suppose the following claims are made by three different groups:

1. The admission policy of Paramount University Medical School systematically discriminates against female and minority applicants; thus it violates affirmative action guidelines.

2. The water in Brown River is polluted and constitutes an acute health hazard for the city's residents.

3. Interplanetary beings have landed and established bases in the remote mountain areas of Wyoming. They are preparing a massive strike against the United States.

A sociologist might feel competent to make a direct assessment of the validity of the first group's assertion, refer the second to a natural scientist, and assert that the claims of the third group are groundless, perhaps investigating the *activities* of this group as an instance of collective delusion. But let us phrase each of these questions differently: is the admission policy of Paramount University a social problem; is water quality of the Brown River a social problem; is the existence of interplanetary visitors a social problem? Phrased in this way, the verification of assertions about conditions is not a fundamental aspect of the sociologist's analysis of social problems. On what theoretical grounds are the facts of some conditions investigated and others dismissed as nonexistent? It would rarely occur to the sociologist to independently attempt to verify the alleged pollution of the river; still less to attempt to objectively confirm a claim about an interplanetary invasion. The fact that the sociologist has become qualified to certify the factual character of *some* claims about conditions does not provide the theoretical warrant for the view that certification of claims is a fundamental feature of social problems analysis. Yet, if the subject matter of social problems is claims-making activity, the *factual basis* of assertions about racist or sexist policies of medical schools is not any more relevant to their status as social problems than the factual basis of assertions about interplanetary invasions.

Two unfortunate consequences follow the sociologists' persistence in addressing the factual existence of imputed conditions as a basis for social problems certification. First, they often mistake their own participation in certifying a very small range of claims for a mandate to make authoritative statements in areas where they have no recognized competence. For example, on what basis can a sociologist claim the authority to comment on the question of the addictive qualities of marijuana or its genetic effects? Second, they inevitably put themselves in the position of borrowing findings from other disciplines whose reliability and validity they cannot evaluate. Richard Fuller, commenting more than a quarter of a century ago, saw clearly that this left the sociologist "open to the charge of professional fakery; i.e., the sociologist took his information and ideas from all the other sciences, and then proceeded to pass moral judgments on what ought to be done." (1938:416) His solution was to abandon the pretense that the sociologist "could hold himself out as an authority on everything from technological unemployment to dementia praecox.... He need not be an expert on social problems, but an expert on the sociology of social problems." (1938:424)

On these grounds, it is not such an extreme position to urge that sociologists of social problems set aside the issue of the objective basis of alleged conditions, even to the extent of remaining indifferent to their existence. Does this mean that we maintain such conditions do not exist, or that the sociologist or any other scientist should not attempt to document their existence and study their causes? Not at all. Whatever the factual basis of the various conditions imputed to exist, the claims-making and responding activities themselves are the subject matter of the sociology of social problems. We contend that these activities exist, and can be documented and analyzed from a sociological perspective.

CLAIMS-MAKING ACTIVITIES

The activity of making claims, complaints, or demands for change is the core of what we call social problems activities. Definitions of conditions as social problems are constructed by members of a society who attempt to call attention to situations they find repugnant and who try to mobilize the institutions to do something about them.

The dictionary defines a claim as:

1. an authoritative or challenging request;
2. a demand of a right or supposed right;
3. a calling on another for something due, or supposed to be due;
4. an assertion, statement or implication often made, or likely to be suspected of being made, without adequate justification. (Webster's New International Dictionary, 3d ed., s.v. "claim.")

Claims-making is always a form of interaction: a demand made by one party to another that something be done about some putative condition. A claim implies that the claimant has a right at least to be heard, if not to receive satisfaction. A letter from a constituent to a member of congress urging support of some measure is a claim. So is a petition to the city council to fix potholes in the streets. So, also, is a resolution of a professional body calling for the end of a war in Indochina. Mundanely, claims-making consists of demanding services, filling out forms, lodging complaints, filing lawsuits, calling press conferences, writing letters of protest, passing resolutions, publishing exposés, placing ads in newspapers, supporting or opposing some governmental practice or policy, setting up picket lines or boycotts; these are integral features of social and political life.

All those who involve themselves in these activities participate in the process of defining social problems. As we shall discover, this may include a great variety of persons such as protest groups or moral crusaders who make demands and complaints; the officials or agencies to whom such complaints are directed; members of the media who publicize and disseminate news about such activities (as well as participate in them); commissions of inquiry; legislative bodies and executive or administrative agencies that respond to claims-making constituents; members of the helping professions, such as physicians, psychiatrists, social workers; and sometimes, social scientists who contribute to the definition and development of social problems. Later we will illustrate the participation of each of these groups in social problems activities.

Our definition of social problems cannot be applied by the sociologist without regard to the perspective of the participants who make and respond to claims. That is, the definition does not provide sociologists with a set of criteria that will enable them, "from the outside," to differentiate claims-making from non-claims-making activities. Sociologists' classification of an activity as claims-making is not based on a quality intrinsic to that activity, but rather on the interactional setting in which members make assertions and demands in the name of their right to responsive action. Thus, our definition requires that the sociologist ascertain how *participants* in an activity define that activity.

Usually it is not difficult for the sociologist to recognize and classify activities cited as claims because *they are so recognized and interpreted by members as well.* That is, claims are a common-sense category, understood by members of a society and often associated with such terms as demands, complaints, gripes, and requests.

There are several reasons to stress that the technical term *claim* is also a member's category. However routine and ordinary an event may be, the participants in an activity must construct its meaning as a claim. A complaint presented in the most conventional manner may sometimes be interpreted and dismissed as senseless, just as a bizarre act, such as the delivery of an amputated human ear, may be interpreted as a terrorist's demand for the release of political prisoners. As Horowitz and Liebowitz (1968) have indicated, claims and complaints may be responded to as crime and deviance, implicitly denying their legitimacy, casting them in a different light, and activating an entirely different social institutional response. Or, what might be presented as a claim from the participant's point of view may be defined by institutional authorities as symptoms of mental illness or insanity. Such a construction can effectively defuse the claims-making activity, relegating it to surveillance and control by law enforcement or psychiatric agencies.

Other examples more forcefully demonstrate the socially constructed nature of the category "claim." Activities outside of the usual conventions may be used to make claims, or may be interpreted as claims, whatever their intent. Members may succeed or fail to sustain a definition of these events as an instance of claims-making. For example, a journalist writes a story on the filthy conditions found in the kitchens of local restaurants. While the story neither explicitly criticizes the health department or the proprietors of the restaurants, nor calls for action to be taken, both health officials and proprietors may respond to the charges and demands that they see as implicit in the story. The journalist's reportage is interpreted as a claim.

On the other hand, when firefighters are ambushed by snipers at a fire set to lure them to a particular location, the act my be attributed to or claimed by a local organization. But it may also remain undefined and unclaimed. If the group engaging in such activities issues no communication claiming credit or making demands, on what basis could we say that they were "calling on another for something due"? In such instances, the press, police, and public officials often attempt to make sense of events by attributing them to some known terrorist group. Thus, a claim may be created by observers and added to the actual events in which no claims were, in fact, presented. In the same way, groups may claim credit for an event (a skyjacking, for example) where there is no evidence that they were actually responsible for it.

A number of years ago, in the middle of a class on Eastern religions, a student raised his hand and was called on by the professor. He rose and asked the professor what he thought of the post office. Not understanding the intention or relevance of the question to Eastern religions, the professor returned the question and asked the student what he thought of the post office that he would ask a question about it. The student made a long speech about how inefficient the post office was, citing numerous examples of waste, poor planning, and excess. The most memorable of his examples referred to the safety reflectors on the back doors of large postal trucks. The student informed the class that whereas such trucks may have up to sixteen such reflectors, it was perfectly obvious that two or three at most would have done the same job. The student had with him a large manila file that seemed to contain copious documentation of his outrage, as well as some correspondence with the postal authorities.

The situation created in this class was discomforting and required delicate management on the part of the professor. What was presented as a claim, grievance, or complaint was defined as an instance of bizarre behavior.

Neither the professor of religion nor the students in the class treated the claim as a claim or responded to its content or substance. Nothing about the speech itself, however, would allow an observer to decide that it was not a claim as we have been discussing that term. Had it been addressed to the postal authorities, to the General Accounting Office, or to others who investigate the misuse of funds, those authorities, and therefore the sociologist, would have clearly recognized it as a common type of complaint. This does not preclude that they might not decide later that its author was a crank. The example shows that when the choice of a forum is grossly inappropriate, people making claims will not be treated as claimants, but quite possibly as deranged, misguided, or insane people. It is not possible to predict in advance how such claims will be received, nor to specify which offices are the "appropriate" ones for a given complaint. The example illustrates that proffered claims may be regarded as symptoms, but it does not tell us how to predict when this would occur. Given the emergent and voluntaristic nature of social life, we are not likely ever to be able to make very strict predictive statements of this sort. Perhaps in another class at the same university (a class on social problems?) the speech would have been treated differently.

These marginal cases illustrate that claims are routinely defined by members, not by the sociologist-observer. When members use conventional forms to express complaints and demands, their recognition and registration as claims may be routine. When unconventional forms are used, considerable effort may be expended to define the event as a claim. Some events not intended as claims may be so classified and responded to. Some events intended as claims may be so ambiguous that no one can make much sense of them as such. For example, terrorist activities that threaten to destroy the "fascist insect" may resist any interpretation so that a specific individual or agency could take any action as an accommodative response.

Claims-making most readily brings to mind the demands that crusaders for various social reform and social movements make on governmental agencies and officials. Such activities fall well within our conception of social problems, and we shall occasionally use such examples to illustrate or highlight a point. However, there are a wide variety of other contexts and forums in which social problems claims may be raised. For example, while legislatures have been pressed by activists to decriminalize homosexual acts between consenting adults, the American Psychiatric Association has also responded to demands from within and outside of the profession to declare that homosexuality per se is not an illness. Also, a committee of the American Library Association demanded that the Library of Congress cease classifying books on gay liberation under the heading "sexual perversion." (See Chapter 1.) All of these are examples of social problems claims and provide us with data for the development of a sociology of social problems.

KINDS OF QUESTIONS ABOUT CLAIMS

Having identified and defined a phenomenon for study, what are the questions that need to be asked about this phenomenon, and what kinds of analyses do we propose to make of the data produced by such questions? We shall begin with the consideration of one analytic approach often found in sociological writings that we think is *not* an appropriate or productive line of inquiry.

If we conceived of social problems as claims-making activities, it is apparent that we can easily locate such activities and the people who engage in them in any community or society. We could find the people who write to their congressmen, petition their city council, sign petitions, stage protests, make complaints to local administrative agencies, and so on. One common and seemingly sensible question that comes to mind is: *Why do these people do these things?* What causes people to complain, protest, demand change, join organizations, and lead movements?

When such questions are raised, attention is almost invariably directed toward the individual and social characteristics of those involved and the differences between those who do and those who do not participate in those activities. What background characteristics produce people who join groups, demand change, and engage in protest? When groups or movements are considered the focus of analysis, the characteristics of the leadership role and the social determinants or background characteristics of leaders are often presented.

To study claims-making activities by drawing samples of participants to find individual and social characteristics that predict participation in those activities deflects attention away from the organization of claims-making itself. Since we consider the activities themselves to be the subject matter of social problems, we direct our inquiry to the forms of those activities. We would ask how those activities become organized as they are, rather than why participants become involved in them. We do not mean to say that the latter question is not related to the former, but it is not central to that question. The scores on an authoritarian personality scale of antibusing demonstrators do not inform us how the demonstration was put together, what strategies were used to construct the organization of activities, how the site for the demonstration was chosen, or to what agencies the demonstration was directed.

Returning briefly to our analogy to the sociology of work and occupations, that field does not preoccupy itself with the question, "Why do people work?" Rather, it describes and analyzes how work is organized, asks why it is organized the way it is, or why some work is organized in one way and not another. Similarly, we would ask why social problems activities are organized the way they are, how may variations in organization be accounted for, and why that organization changes over time.

More specifically, what kinds of questions might we ask about claims-making activities? First, let us consider what a claim consists of, what its elemental parts are. A claim is a demand that one party makes upon another. How do these two parties get together so that one is the claimant and the other the recipient of the claim? Second, how does the claimant decide where to lodge a complaint? Given the vast array of jurisdictions, authorities, and referral networks, this selection or funneling process itself is problematic and requires our attention. We cannot take for granted, or begin our analysis with, the claimant and respondent interacting in claims-making activity. Much work has already taken place before they come together. Claimants construct notions about the causes of the conditions they find onerous, assign blame, and locate officials responsible for rectifying the conditions. Alternatively, claimants may decide that no one is in charge of doing something about the condition, and *that* may become the substance of their complaints. Consequently, they may seek out those they think are in charge of creating and assigning such responsibility. Third, they may ask who benefits from the condition in question and look for vested interests—groups that actively perpetuate and profit from it or support it for personal pleasure or convenience. These options, not necessarily mutually exclusive, may lead to different strategies about how the claim should be phrased and to whom it should be directed.

Let us examine the other side: the various agencies to whom claims are directed selectively encourage or discourage various kinds of claims. Many such agencies are mandated to serve the public, to answer their complaints, and to solve their problems. Handling claims is their business. Sometimes this business is fairly competitive, sometimes it is monopolistic. Agencies and their personnel may sometimes attempt to enlarge the scope of their mandate, increase their budgets, and expand their horizons. One way of doing this is to cultivate more business, or to encourage a wider variety of clients to seek their services. An agency can make the claims-making process more inviting and present itself to various publics as a problem-solving organization. Some kinds of claimants are more desirable than others. Agencies may discourage claims from low-status persons, from groups who will not be grateful for their services, and from groups that will not be easily satisfied by what the agency is prepared to do.

Agencies have their own idea of the work they are authorized to do and the clientele who can legitimately demand their services. They may agree or refuse to recognize, accept, or register the proffered claim. Any of a variety of factors may influence them to weigh their authority and discretion, interpret their mandate, and finally, to include or exclude a claim from their jurisdiction. People's complaints about noxious odors in their neighborhood may pass through a long referral network in search of an agency willing to accept and take charge of it. Sometimes none is found, and the complaint goes unheeded. In the process, the actual substance of the claim may change, refocused to make it appear to be the work of whatever agency or office is approached. For example, if mental health facilities are installed in a community, complaints that might previously have been directed to the police and become law enforcement problems may instead be phrased as problems of mental health. This may happen not only because community mental health workers respond to complaints in this way, but because people present their complaints as problems of mental health in order to get the agency to respond to them.

Such examples suggest that there is no simple, mechanical, causal relationship between a condition, the experiences of dissatisfaction with the condition, and the activation of responses to complaints. Indeed, the conventional argument that troublesome, disruptive, or dysfunctional conditions create dissatisfactions which, in turn, activate institutional responses can be reversed. The establishment of an agency authorized to deal with certain conditions generates dissatisfactions among populations about conditions that previously were unseen or routinely accommodated. That is, the awareness of availability of services leads to definitions of—and activity about—conditions as troublesome or disruptive.

There are two issues that are implicitly expressed in this argument. The first concerns the contingencies in the process of getting claims established and registered with some responding agency. Variations in dissatisfaction cannot account for the variable ways that those dissatisfactions are expressed, acted upon, or responded to by others. Deprivation or exploitation or even starvation cannot account for how a specific group of people formulate their troubles or to whom they turn for redress. (Blumer, 1971, makes this point at some length.)

The second, more unconventional, issue draws on the conception that solutions produce problems by providing the framework within which those problems can be stated. Many writers on social problems have said that the belief that something could be done about a condition is a prerequisite to its becoming a social problem. People do not define as problems those conditions they feel are immutable, inherent in human nature, or the will of God. Nor can it be assumed that dissatisfaction or outrage is either natural or to be taken for granted. Every experience of displeasure and dissatisfaction has its origins in the availability, if not promise, of remedies, cures, reforms, and solutions for such troubles. Those who promulgate standards and who claim expertise and healing methods may suggest that conditions previously thought to be unchangeable or part of human nature can be ameliorated. By defining, giving a name to, and developing a theory to account for this trouble, they make it possible for others to experience as unsatisfactory some aspect of their environment that previously they had been unaware of. Everett Hughes has eloquently analyzed the relation between experienced dissatisfactions and those who define and make them possible.

Persons and organizations have problems. They want things done for them, for their bodies and souls, for their social and financial relations, for their cars, houses, bridges, sewage systems. They want things done to the people they consider their competitors or their enemies. What they want done no doubt has some existence apart from the system of services within which the professions operate, but we scarcely know what their problems would be, that is, in what circumstances they would think they had problems, how they would define the problems, to whom they would turn for help, what they would offer in return for it, what they would consider good service, and what recourse they would have if the service were not satisfactory. It is in the course of interaction with one another and with the professionals that the problems of people are given definition. Pains and complaints are the lot of the human (and other) species. But diseases are inventions. They are definitions of conditions and situations. Professionals do not merely serve. They define the very wants they serve. Thus, the old dictum that the professionals fulfill the basic wants or desires of people and society is much too simple. (Hughes, 1971:422)

The dissatisfactions that provide the content and perceived basis for claims are the products of interaction between those who become claimants—clients or patients—and those who provide the vocabularies of discomfort and the possibilities of alternative solutions. Solutions, as well as conditions, are putative. Only the prior existence of these institutional arrangements and putative solutions make problems possible, perceptible, nameable, and actionable.

We shall return to these issues in the next chapter. They are mentioned here to indicate the kinds of questions that get lost when analysis turns prematurely to the etiology of claims-making activity. To focus on the causes of claims-making activities at the outset deflects attention away from the phenomenon itself. This results in a failure to discover and develop the basic characteristics of the activity sufficiently to determine just what issues we might want to subject to etiological analysis.

THE ROLE OF VALUES

Earlier, we showed how Fuller and Myers utilized the concept of values in their account of the definitional process, and how their use of this concept shifted their analytic focus from the definitions of conditions to the *causes* of conditions. Value judgments, as Fuller and Myers pointed out, lead people to experience conditions as offensive and to define them as social problems. Social problems activities are heavily freighted with morality and values. People making claims often express indignation, phrasing their claims as demands for more equitable, orderly, humane, or convenient arrangements. Claims are normative phenomena. They are statements about conditions that *ought not* to exist; something *ought* to be done to improve conditions. The concept of values, therefore, is clearly relevant for the analysis of social problems. Surprisingly, there is almost no literature on moral indignation, as such. The two works ritually cited by sociologists (Scheler, 1961, and Ranulf, 1938) provide little guidance for sociologists using this concept.

The use of values to explain individual behavior is well established in sociological theory and analysis. There is also a tradition of dissent which poses two objections to such formulations. (Bott, 1968; Matza, 1969; Lemert, 1967; Homans, 1967:12-13; Barnett, 1954; Liebow, 1967) First, values are vested with the power to produce effects beyond empirical justification. In Lemert's words:

> *The common tendency is to reify what can be no more than a mental construct and to give it properties appropriate to an order of phenomena different from that which it describes.... i.e., in Merton's usage, culture "defines, regulates and controls". . . the empirically more tenable alternative is that only human beings define, regulate and control behavior of other human beings. (1967:5)*

In addition, the use of values or culture as an independent variable is inevitably compromised by a tautology between the values and the behavior it is meant to explain.

> *To say that people behave differently, or have different expectations because they belong to different cultures (i.e., have different values) amounts to no more than saying that they behave differently because they behave differently, or that cultures are different because they are different. (Bott, 1968:219)*

The use of values to explain why people define conditions as social problems is an explanation by fiat; it avoids addressing an important empirical issue, i.e., *how* and *by what process* do values produce such effects? If we wish to explain why people define a condition as a social problem, we may observe them making demands for the amelioration of some condition they find offensive. That is, we find them asserting value judgments and arguing for positions based on them. We may also find them competing with, resisting, and attacking opposing groups. What do we add if we explain this behavior by saying that people's values make them do these things? First, our inference that people have values, or that different groups have different values, is drawn from the very behavior we wish to explain in the first place. We observe people acting differently. We infer they have different values. Then we use these values to explain why they are acting differently.

There are two solutions to these problems, one, a "reasonable" compromise position, the other a more extreme view. The reasonable solution accepts the notion that social problems are activities of individuals and groups. To ask what are the effective causes of social problems, or what keeps social problems activities going, is to ask what sustains the participants in these activities. Some groups may be led to the social problems arena through moral indignation, for example, humanitarian reformers, crusaders of various persuasion, and garden-variety "do-gooders." However, not all social problems activities spring from this sort of disinterested, principled activity. Humanitarian crusaders by definition set out to improve the lot of disadvantaged others. They are not themselves victims of the conditions they set out to ameliorate. When those who complain *claim to be* the victims of the conditions, we call them an *interest group*. Thus, interest groups are those who claim to have something to gain or lose over and above the way everyone else in a society might be affected. For example, in their efforts to decriminalize homosexual acts, the Gay Activists Alliance is involved in legislative processes as an interest group, while legal, church, and other organizations in support of such legislation do so on disinterested, principled grounds.

In this regard, our formulation bears a similarity to the so-called group approach to politics exemplified in the classic formulations of Bentley (1908) and Truman (1951). It is instructive to contrast Truman's definition of interest groups with our distinction between interest groups and disinterested, or value-oriented, groups. Truman defines interest groups as

> ...*any group, that on the basis of one or more shared attitudes, makes certain claims upon other groups in the society for the establishment, maintenance or enhancement of forms of behavior that are implied by the shared attitudes. These shared attitudes [deai with] what is needed or wanted in a given situation, observable as demands or claims upon other groups in the society. The shared attitudes, moreover, constitute the interests. (1951:33-4)*

Truman's definition is much broader than our own conception and would include both interested and disinterested groups. We define interest as *any real and material advantage or stake that an individual or group claims, or ıs imputed by others to have, in the outcome of activity.* The scope of this definition is intentionally broad to suggest that almost any aspect or object in social life may become the focal point for social problems activity. Not all groups that enter the social problems arena do so to defend some interest; their impetus may be altruistic. Similarly, not all activities of interest groups are directed toward defining social problems. For example, a significant portion of the work of the National Association for the Advancement of Colored People, a group that is frequently involved in claims-making activity, deals with organizational problems as raising funds for scholarships, recruiting members, and planning their annual convention.

Groups defining conditions as social problems may be sustained by interests or values, or a combination of them. Some of the interesting varieties might include the following:

1. Value groups may find that as they raise a condition as a social problem, they gain as allies other groups who have a vested interest in their claim.

2. Interest groups may find that public debate must take place in terms of values or ideals. Thus, in order to present claims effectively or argue a position, groups must acquire a set of values that legitimate their claims. Clinical psychologists, pressing their claims against the psychiatric profession's monopoly over the practice of psychotherapy, may find their case strengthened by a statement of their concern about the lack of attention and service given to the mental health of the poor.

3. A protest group may find a convenient overlap between their interest and their publicly espoused values. That is, their claims as an interest group are easily articulated with statements of values to legitimate those claims. An adoption agency concerned about the encroachment onto their domain of other organizations is able to espouse the importance of professional counseling services for unmarried mothers in the adoption process, services that only this agency may be organized and staffed to provide.

4. Alternatively, a group may find itself cross-pressured when its interest requires it to sacrifice or ignore some publicly stated value, or its values may require it to work against its own interests. School administrators who are doctrinally committed to integrated education sometimes find themselves compromising these values while opposing school bussing in the name of "orderly" educational processes.

5. To the extent that a disinterested, value-oriented group is successful in its activity, it may develop various interests to protect: organizations, careers, reputations. It may face a crisis of the "routinization of disinterest" when others charge they are self-serving, rather than altruistic. An anticruelty-to-animals group may be reluctant to investigate charges that pet-shop owners who contribute money to their organization fail to maintain health standards in the care of the animals they sell.

The reasonable or compromise view makes a distinction between interested and value-oriented social problems activities. This goes beyond the bald assertion that value judgments cause people to define conditions as social problems. It provides a place for pure, value-driven participants while, at the same time, it allows that many engaged in social problems activities are there to defend vested interests. In addition, it provides for the possibility that groups may disingenuously espouse value positions and take pragmatic views to protect their interests. Values and interests constitute rival or complementary explanations of the activities of social problem groups or individuals.

However, this compromise formulation contains difficulties. It leads the sociologist to make certain inferences that are difficult to document. Given that most social problems participants express moral positions, how would the sociologist separate those who are sincere, thus driven by value positions, from those who are cynically manipulating values to pursue their own material interests? The view that values and interests are rival causes of social problems activities leads to insoluble methodological difficulties when it comes to applying these concepts to empirical situations. For example, a professional group took a position against no-fault divorce. Representatives of this group argued that the no-fault procedures do not protect the interests of third parties because the new procedures eliminate serious judicial review and examination of the agreement. Children of parents divorced in this manner are not adequately represented and are often left in an ambiguous position with respect to their property or care. The association documented cases where extreme neglect resulted from no-fault divorce and pleaded that the children not be sacrificed for the sake of procedural simplifications for the parents. Is such a group engaged in the disinterested moral crusade devoted to the care of neglected children? This is, in fact, the position of an association of divorce attorneys who stand to lose a significant part of their practice as a consequence of the institution of no-fault divorce. Does the source of this plea for the protection of children change the status of this group from value-oriented to interested social problems group? Would it compel the sociologist to shift the analysis or diagnosis of the causes of the claims-making activity in this case?

The example clearly indicates that causal analyses, after all, do presuppose a model of human conduct, one in which motives are constructed and imputed to individuals and groups. While most sociologists would be reluctant to engage directly in imputing motives, some might make use of a formulation that implicitly incorporates such imputations. To apply the distinction between value-oriented and interested activities, the sociologist would somehow have to be able to ascertain whether the divorce attorneys, in this case, were disinterested, altruistic professionals or cynical lawyers intent on maintaining a client population by "using children as a political football."

Joseph Gusfield presents a serious discussion of this problem in his book, *Symbolic Crusade.* Gusfield documents and interprets a social problem in terms of a larger set of interests that shaped the activities of participants, although they themselves might have been unable to describe those interests. Gusfield argues that the temperance and later the prohibition movements were vehicles through which rival groups in nineteenth-century America sought to symbolize which groups dominated society. The issue of drinking alcoholic beverages divided the society between the old Protestant natives and the newer Catholic immigrants who were filling up the cities and gradually making their mark on American politics. The final victory of prohibition in 1919 was a symbolic victory for the old, but declining, rural-based, elite group. It had lost all of the important battles but had won, at least temporarily, a symbolic victory. In effect, Gusfield argues that when various groups were contending over the issue of who should be allowed to drink what kind of alcohol, they were in fact engaged in a struggle for political dominance.

In a short section entitled "A Note on Religious Motives and Sociological Reductionism," Gusfield discusses the objections to his thesis:

> *Historians are likely to register an objection to our mode of analysis. They are apt to accuse us of the sociological error of reductionism. The argument might be advanced that in emphasizing the functions of Temperance for the social structure, we have distorted the importance of religious and moral motives in a movement that aimed to bring men to a higher level of moral perfection. . . . Religious compulsion drove men to build a more perfect world because it was right, not because it was instrumental. Duty, not utility, played a major hand in the reformist upsurge. When the sociologist finds economic or social considerations at work, he is often accused of having "reduced" religious motives to self-interested status needs. Temperance is, as we have admitted, the offspring of religious revivalism. The process of "reduction" hides and belittles the fact, or so the argument would run. (1963:57)*

Having anticipated this criticism, Gusfield responded by distinguishing functional from descriptive analyses:

> *The charge of reductionism implies that the reducer finds the claims of his subjects to disinterested benevolence to be false ones. It suggests that we see religion as a "front" behind which men stalk after power, status and income. This fails to appreciate the sociologist's concern for functional, rather than descriptive questions. . . .*

> *A function of Temperance activities was to enhance the symbolic properties of liquor and abstinence as marks of status. This is not an assertion that this was its only function, nor is it an assertion about motives. It merely points out that as a consequence of such activities, abstinence became symbolic of a status level. (1963:59)*

Gusfield is not unwilling to attribute motives to his subject. He acknowledges "religious compulsions," as well as instrumental interests, as rival causes of the activities he wishes to explain. He is, however, unwilling to describe the moral crusaders as sincere in their efforts "to bring men to a higher level of moral perfection." He does not wish to describe their activities as a cynically motivated pursuit of vested interests, status, or power. He claims that functional analysis provides an alternative that denies neither values, nor vested interests as valid causes by invoking a different level of analysis. Whatever values or interests may have motivated the contending groups, the function of their activities was to express their struggle for political dominance.

What is implied, but left out on the functional interpretation, is an account of how the participants constructed and imputed motives to the various groups. While the analyst might shy away from imputing motives, participants do not. In the process of defining a condition as a social problem, one of the constituent activities is the construction and imputation of motives to the major figures involved. Whether the crusader is Ralph Nader, Barry Commoner, Neal Dow, or Lyman Beecher, we may expect a questioning and probing of the motives of those who seek to enforce moral rules on others. Members of society assess the sincerity of the crusaders and, in the process, decide whether they are value-oriented in their commitment, represent interest groups, or are "ego-tripping" and "playing to the media." Such assessments of motives, how they are constructed by participants, and how they serve to explain activities are data for the sociological analyst. We cannot interpret those motives as anything other than imputations made by participants; they tell us nothing about the "real" motives that presumably energize those activities.

Our discussion of interests and values has been influenced by C. Wright Mill's (1940) classic treatment of motives. He took issue with the conventional conception of motives as explanations of social conduct. In this view, motives are conventionally thought of as prime movers or springs to action lying deep within the individual. For this reason they are considered difficult to identify, and the "real" motives of an act are not easily accessible, even to the individuals whose conduct is shaped by them. Thus, the study of motives has come to be the province of specialists—psychologists, psychoanalysts, or sociologists— trained to determine the "real" motives, as opposed to the superficial or shallow reasons that members might give to explain their actions. People are said to be only dimly aware of their values, to take them for granted, or to apply them unknowingly. Social analysts who use values as explanations stress that values are learned, that these values are internalized during the socialization process, particularly in early childhood when basic values are implanted in the individual. Other analysts may stress adult socialization or more situational determinants, but however they are internalized, implanted, or learned, those values and motives guide and determine human conduct.

Mills called this mode of analysis *motive-mongering* and doubted that it could produce any significant explanation to account for social conduct. He proposed, instead, a radically different conception of motives and, by implication, values. Motives, he said, are the answers people give to the question,

"Why did you do that?" They are attempts to justify or to explain a line of conduct that has been questioned. Scott and Lyman (1968) and Blum and McHugh (1971) have more recently developed this conception of motives. When no questions are raised about a line of conduct, that is, when its meaning is not made problematic either by the actor or any member of her audience, the motivation of her acts is not a feature of her interaction with others. Motives, then, are a product of a member's activity to explain problematic conduct. They are a kind of resource available in the language and culture of groups for use when certain kinds of questions arise; specifically, questions about the meaning or purpose of some line of activity. Motives are used by people to reestablish meaning and to restore the flow of interaction that has been interrupted or put into questions.

Mills further suggested that this line of argument undercuts the assertion that every action has a unique motive, for motives are shaped and patterned by linguistic and cultural resources. Furthermore, since motives are conceived to be answers to questions about actions *after the fact,* they cannot have been causes of those acts. Thus, any number of answers, or motives, are possible in a given situation. The motive used may vary according to who asks the question—a policeman, clergyman, husband, son, employer, or friend may construct quite different answers to the question, "Why did you do that?" Mills coined the phrase "the vocabulary of motives" to refer to these choices and suggested that such vocabularies represent the variety of motives a person may choose from when asked, "Why did you do that?" These vocabularies may change over time as motives become discredited as explanations or new justifications for certain acts are devised. For example, in the wake of the women's liberation movement, biophysiological motives as an explanation for the failure of women to apply for certain occupational positions are vigorously rejected by activists in favor of sociopolitical motives. Finally, Mills' analysis makes no assumptions or assertions about the sincerity of personal avowals of motives. An analyst could never tell if a person were really sincere in stating a motive. Further, such questions have little relevance for analyzing the process of how meanings are reestablished in problematic situations.

We use Mills' treatment of motives to reconceptualize the role of values in social problems activities. Values are the explanations people give in support of their claims, complaints, or demands. Claims are commonly buttressed by espousals of moral positions, assertions of value judgments, and expressions of indignation or outrage. Claims-makers do not simply say, "We want you to change this." They say, "It's not right that this should be happening! This is wrong! This is unjust, unfair, and violates our rights! This condition is disgusting and should not be allowed! People who engage in such practices should be institutionalized! Why? Because it's un-American; it's against religion; it's debasing, degrading, humiliating, unwholesome, exploitative, dangerous, and irresponsible."

Claims express demands within a moral universe. Values are those statements that express *the grounds or the basis* of the complaint. They are used to justify a demand, to explain not simply what is wrong, but why it is wrong. Like motives, values are a resource in the language; they are used to justify a line of conduct. In social problems, values are invoked to justify claims or demands, or express dissatisfaction, indignation, or outrage. They are answers to the questions, "Why does this make you angry?" or, "What's wrong with the way we handle this now?" Viewed in this way, values are part of the data of social problems rather than explanations of them. To say that social problems activities are heavily freighted with values is not to say that values cause social problems, or that values lead people to define conditions as problems. Rather, values are a constituent feature of social problems activities that are observable in what participants do and say.

Just as there are vocabularies of motives, so there may be a wide choice of values that may be used to articulate a claim. These may be chosen very strategically according to the agency, organization, or institution to which the claim is directed. Strategy in the choice of values may rest on an analysis of the previous success of phrasing a complaint in specified ways. For example, a group protesting the firing of a popular professor might debate whether they should phrase their claim as a question of academic freedom, civil liberties, racism, sexism, or due process. Each of these is a value position that might be used to legitimate a particular claim. None are inherent in the event that activated their protest; thus, none are the cause of its definition as a problem. Vocabularies of values to express dissatisfactions provide participants with a range of choices, choices that are not mechanically determined by the condition itself.

Alvin Gouldner developed this line of thought in a discussion of the "language of morality." The logic of his analysis and the conclusions to which it leads are worth summarizing and comparing with our view:

I shall begin by approaching the problem of the sources of morality on the most general level. The language of morality—hence morality, itself, for it is not accessible to study, except through its linguistic manifestation—arises in the social world in situations where what men want, *the gratifications they seek, are precarious and uncertain. The crux of the whole matter is that morality is rooted in the scarcity and contingency of desired objects or performances.... We begin, thus, with this deliberately simplified model in which "ego" wants "0" from "alter."* Why *he wants "0" is irrelevant here. Ego will make imputations about alter both in terms of whether alter is* willing *to do as ego wants, and* second, *whether he is* able *to do so. . . . I shall also assume that ego simply dichotomizes his imputations: he assumes that alter is either willing or unwilling, able or unable. From this simplified standpoint four possibilities emerge. (1970:266)*

Three of these do not call forth the notion of morality. Gouldner says that the possibilities "neither willing nor able," "both willing and able," and "willing but unable" require no particular action. In the first and third cases, having defined "alter" as unable, "ego" would consider persuasion to achieve the desired end fruitless; in the second, since he is considered "willing," no persuasion is needed to convince an able "alter."

The fourth possible situation brings us to the heart of the matter. Ego may view alter as able but unwilling to do as he wants. Here ego will attempt to influence alter in some manner, by exhortation or command, or by supplying incentives or punishments, or by threatening or promising to do so.

It is primarily in this situation I would suggest that the language and sentiments of morality—"ought" and "should" arise and are most fully developed and used. Morality and moral claims are one basic way in which ego can get alter to do as he wants. (We view morality as emerging in situations in which there is a scarcity or contingency of desired performances or objects, and when this is defined by ego as due to alter's unwillingness to provide them, rather than to his lack of skill, competence or resources and facilities. Faced with someone who is able, but unwilling to do as he wishes and against whom his own power and his own ability to promise benefits or threaten punishments is always at some point limited, ego must find a way to modify alter's motives that does not depend upon the benefits or punishment he can provide.) This must then take the form of some "appeal" that, on the one hand, is not narrowly situational, and on the other, is not related to promised benefits or threatened punishments. This is essentially the character of moral language. It is not situational, for it always refers to what should be done in a type of situation by a type of person. There is no moral claim that is incumbent on only one specific person in only one concrete instance. . . . Morality is a rhetoric ego uses to mobilize alter's motives for complying with his wants, without express reference to the manner in which the situation will be changed by improved benefits, or by avoided costs. It defocalizes situational consequences. It implies that these are not relevant to the decision to do or not do what is sought. On the one side, it implies that alter should do something, regardless of whether or not he will gain or lose from it. On the other, when ego demands conformity with a moral claim, he is intimating that he is not doing so because of any partisan interest or any personal advantage he will derive if alter complies. The social function of the language of morality, then, is to induce action without exercise of power or compulsion and apart from the offering of rewards. (Gouldner, 1970:266-273)

Gouldner's formulation displays many similarities to Mills' treatment of motives and values and our adaptation of it. First, he emphasizes their linguistic and rhetorical character. Morality is a *way of talking* and must be understood as such. Second, the use of rhetoric of morality is contingent on the *imputation* by ego that alter is able, but unwilling to assist him. It is not a question of whether alter is actually or really able, but unwilling to assist, but ego's imputation of those conditions that leads to the use of the language of morality. Third, Gouldner indicates that ego's use of the language of morality transforms his personal wants into a moral claim on alter by presenting his demand as one who does so without prospect of personal advantage and without partisan interest. This presupposes that alter accords ego the status of disinterested party and acknowledges the legitimacy of the claim per se. Thus, as instruments for the solution of conditions defined as problems, the rhetoric of morality generalizes personal experiences into social issues by casting them in terms of a shared linguistic community.

Gouldner's careful attention to language here parallels our own efforts to focus on how ego imputes or decides to use moral persuasion, rather than an analysis of which members of society actually could help if only they would. Pressing the logic of this analysis, we may reassess the reasonable or compromise argument that both values and interests provide sociologists with causal explanations of social problems activities. Our examination of how members use language to make sense of their own, as well as others', activities leads us to the view that *neither* values nor interests may be considered causes of those activities. Members of a society make imputations about the sincerity or lack of it when people espouse moral positions, and *they* may conclude that values or morals are adequate grounds to explain a given line of conduct. Similarly, members may look for vested interests hidden beneath seemingly principled positions. When they find such interests, they may subsequently attribute actions to these influences, or they may not. Values and interests explain conduct to participants, not to the sociologist of social problems. This process of imputation is itself an important element of the subject matter for the sociologist; it is a fundamental aspect of the definitional process that the sociologist should study.

SUMMARY

In this chapter we have introduced a conception of social problems and attempted to elaborate a definition of the activities around which we feel a vigorous, substantive area of study might develop. We took as our model the study of work and occupations, a substantive area that provides us with a methodology to recast our definition of social problems to avoid logical and terminological problems in empirical research. This led us to abandon the notion that social problems are a kind of condition. We chose, instead, to identify a class of activities to define our subject matter. This strategy permits empirical analysis whenever even a single member of the class of activities is identified, so that, for example, the study of prostitution is logically as uncomplicated for the sociologist of social problems as for the sociologist of occupations.

We have defined social problems activities as claims-making, complaints, and demands for the relief and amelioration of offensive conditions. In elaborating on this definition, we clearly distinguish between claims made about the condition and the condition itself. The term putative conditions is used to indicate the focus of our interest in the member's claims without regard to their validity. We also emphasize that the construction of definitions of conditions, the expression of claims, and the imputation of motives and values are the activities of members, and all are part of the phenomena of social problems to be studied.

Finally, we attempted to clarify the kinds of questions that might be asked about the activities we define as social problems. We specifically urge that certain kinds of questions, common to both public concern and positivistic sociology, be set aside. Premature consideration of the causes of any phenomenon turns attention to the supposed antecedents of the activity, rather than to the activity itself. This concern for explaining social conduct in terms of the motives and values that activate it leads to mistaking the data of analysis for the analysis itself. In the effort to identify, measure, and analyze motives and values, sociologists have often confused their own constructions with those of the participants. Indeed, they often ignore the members' constructions of motives and values altogether. As a consequence, the study of social problems misconceives or ignores how values and motives are employed by members in the process of defining social problems.

We have attempted to clarify this misconception by examining Mills' analysis of motives and Gouldner's formulation of the language of morality. This has led us to the view that values are one of the resources members use in their efforts to define conditions as social problems. While members may impute motives, values, or interests to explain the conduct of other participants in social problems activities, such concepts cannot provide sociologists with explanations for they are themselves part of the phenomenon that must be described and explained.

6

The Description and Analysis of
Social Problems Activities:
An Extended Empirical Example

The bulk of this chapter is devoted to a detailed empirical example of social problems activities, a controversy that developed out of efforts to publicize the use of psychiatry to control political dissidents in the Soviet Union. No single case, however detailed, is ever representative of a general class of events, but any well-developed case may provide the opportunity to illustrate broader theoretical issues.

SOCIAL PROBLEMS AS ACTIVITIES: WHAT WOULD
THE RESEARCH LOOK LIKE ?

In his essay on revolutions in science, Thomas Kuhn stated that those who propose a new paradigm do two things. First, they focus attention on new kinds of questions, setting aside the ingrown controversies of the prevailing paradigm and the "normal" science it sponsors. Second, they establish a procedure for examining these new questions; that is, they present an *exemplar* or model that shows how the new questions lead to and demand new data, research skills, and techniques.

> *By it [exemplars] I mean, initially, the concrete problem-solutions that students encounter from the start of their scientific education, whether in laboratories, on examinations, or at the ends of chapters in science texts. To these shared examples should be added at least some of the technical problem-solutions found in the periodical literature that scientists encounter during their post-educational research careers and that also show them by example how their job is to be done. More than other sorts of components of the disciplinary matrix, differences between sets of exemplars provide the community fine-structure of science. (1970:187)*

Those proposing new paradigms do not always provide such exemplars. Without this leadership, supporters and critics may conclude that the new paradigm is simply a reinterpretation of existing data, not a demand for new kinds of data. As a consequence, it may simply be assimilated into the existing theoretical orthodoxy.

Even when an exemplar or research model is presented, there is no assurance that it, in fact, will be closely related to the theoretical formulation to which it is appended, or that the model will be expanded or elaborated in a methodologically consistent direction. This may be illustrated by the contrast between the empirical and theoretical chapters in Howard Becker's *Outsiders.* The first three chapters of the book present an original and distinctive paradigm for the study of those who construct and react to deviance. However, four of the five empirical chapters that follow them do not present research on the societal reaction to deviance, but are concerned with the deviants themselves. The unconventional treatment of deviants presented in these chapters gives the impression that they were the kinds of research recommended by the novel theoretical paradigm. As exemplars for a theory of societal reaction, the studies are misleading. They have directed attention to the acts of deviants, albeit from the perspective of those deviants, rather than to the activities of those who define and treat them as such.

This is a common pattern of so-called innovations in the field of social problems. Some innovations have proved to be simply an updated terminology replacing terms that have become antiquated or tainted by moral judgments. The replacement of the term *social pathology* by *social disorganization* was in part such a change. It was also a more sophisticated and less vulgar statement of the same kind of theory. Likewise, when the term *deviant behavior* succeeded *personal disorganization,* it produced no exemplars to generate new data. While the introductions and conclusions of social problems texts may change, reflecting terminological fads and fashions, the chapters in the middle continue to address the same subjects, present the same kinds of data (organized for the most part in statistical form), and use the same modes of analysis.

The value-conflict formulation of social problems did call for new kinds of data to accompany the shift of attention from the "objective conditions" to the process by which putative conditions are perceived, defined, and treated as problems. But this research tradition did not develop, perhaps because of logical inconsistencies in the theory itself.

The value-conflict formulation has also been absorbed into the existing orthodoxy as a competing interpretation or explanation of traditional subject matter. It has been cast as a social-psychological theory of social problems in which values or value conflicts are invoked to explain the conventional list of social evils—delinquency, racial prejudice, urban blight, and prostitution. Occasionally, the value-conflict view is discussed in opposition to the prevalent disorganization theory: sometimes it is one element of an eclectic formulation

(Horton and Leslie, 1965; Cuber and Harper, 1948), and other times it is treated simply as one of many approaches to social problems. (Lemert, 1968; Rubington and Weinberg, 1971)

New research models are more difficult to present than new theories. If a new theory is merely a reinterpretation of existing data, then only the introduction and conclusions of a textbook, along with certain key terms, must be changed. The bulk of the material remains the same. In a field where most authors write for undergraduate students and produce weighty textbooks, this is far easier and more practical than to attempt to follow a new theory into areas where knowledge and research findings are not already conveniently organized and packaged. A genuinely new paradigm will, by definition, reconceptualize the traditional subject matter and require new methodologies and research techniques to produce new kinds of data. These are so difficult to assemble that most innovators in social problems, eyeing the textbook market, make marginal innovations within the existing orthodoxy.

Our attempt is to define a field of research, and to this end we address the questions: What kinds of data does a social definitional approach to social problems lead to? How would you study social problems in this way? What would the data look like? The case materials that constitute the bulk of this chapter are, we believe, the data for an analysis of social problems activities. The methods used—library research, the analysis of documents, and unstructured interviews with elites—while rare in previous social problems research, are well-established tools in other social science disciplines. Thus, no great retooling is required to study social problems, nor are the required materials obscure or inaccessible. Any graduate student or advanced undergraduate could have assembled the same data.

Following Kuhn's injunction that a proposed new paradigm offers an example to show how the new questions generated by the paradigm lead to new data, research agendas, and analytic techniques, we present an example of claims-making activity. The data are in a detailed and raw form. We know that the detail may sometimes be burdensome or bewildering, but we do this to illustrate the distinctive kinds of data required for documenting claims-making activity. Our commentary and interpretations of these data will be identified as such under separate headings.

In the following presentation of data, excerpts from published books and articles are cited in the usual style of scholarly notation. All other quotes and references are fully identified in the text. These include official actions of the American Psychiatric Association, whether published in the "official business" section of the *American Journal of Psychiatry (AJP)* or in *Psychiatric News,* letters to the editors of journals or newspapers, or newspaper articles. Unpublished documents are also identified in the text, including minutes to meetings, memos, letters, research proposals, and excerpts from interviews conducted by the senior author.

SOCIAL PROBLEMS IN THE AMERICAN PSYCHIATRIC ASSOCIATION: A CASE STUDY

In January of 1971, Vladimir Bukovsky, a twenty-nine-year-old dissident Soviet biologist, sent to England the secret psychiatric dossiers of six Soviet dissidents he said were being held in Soviet mental hospitals because of their political beliefs. In a letter accompanying the documents, published in *The Times,* Bukovsky asked:

> *I realize that at a distance and without the essential clinical information it is very difficult to determine the mental condition of a person, and either to diagnose an illness or assert the absence of any illness. Therefore, I ask you to express your opinion on only one point: Do the above mentioned diagnoses contain enough scientifically based evidence, not only to indicate the mental illness described in the diagnoses, but also to indicate the necessity of isolating these people completely from society? (March 12, 1971)*

This was probably the first look that Westerners had at clinical diagnostic files of Soviet political dissidents. But it was not the first report reaching the West of how psychiatry is used to control politically active Soviet citizens, nor the first effort to involve Western psychiatrists and their professional associations in the controversy over the use and misuse of psychiatry for political ends.

In March 1970, a letter to the editor of the *American Journal of Psychiatry* noted the case of Major General Peter G. Grigorenko, who had been arrested, charged with anti-Soviet activity, and declared insane after being examined at the Serbsky Institute of Psychiatry in Moscow. The author, a native of Poland who worked as a psychiatrist in Russia during World War II, described similar incidents from that period and called for:

> *. . . some action on behalf of General Grigorenko, either through the U.N. Commission on Human Rights, or through the World Psychiatric Association, which has many Communist satellite countries as members.*
>
> *The shame of Soviet psychiatry should be exposed to the whole free world. Perhaps through pressure by the psychiatric community of the free world, the lot of political "patients" suffering from "counter-revolutionary delusions" can be helped. (AJP, 126:9, p. 1327; see also letter of December 1970: AJP, 127:6, pp. 842-3)*

The documentation was, however, thin. None of the supposedly sane people had been examined by outside psychiatrists. In a profession where it is not accepted practice for one to evaluate the decision of another without such an examination and supporting tests and evaluations, it is not surprising that someone else raised questions about the allegations of misuse and incarceration of sane individuals. The second author, who had taken a tour of some Soviet psychiatric facilities, questioned Soviet colleagues on the point:

> *When I persisted that we kept hearing of artists, writers, and others being put into mental institutions because of their anti-Soviet statements, he asked me how I knew that these persons were not psychotic. He pointed out that the incidence of schizophrenia among the artistically gifted is not particularly low. It occurred to me that the ranks of political dissenters, in the Soviet Union as elsewhere, might contain at least a fair share of schizophrenia, too. . . . [in regard to Grigorenko] How does "an Observer" [the author of the first letter] know he was not mentally ill? (AJP, 127:11. p. 1575)*

In December 1970, before the Bukovsky documentation had left the Soviet Union, the Section on Psychiatry of the British Columbia Medical Association recommended to the Canadian Psychiatric Association a resolution "calling for further study and actions regarding such alleged practices in the USSR, or in any other country or countries where similar practices are alleged to take place." In January 1971 the Canadian Psychiatric Association accepted the resolution and urged the Canadian Medical Association to study the report and to raise the issue in medical associations of other countries, international psychiatric organizations, the World Health Organization, and the World Psychiatric Association. It commented that the "information concerning instances of such practices included in the report is as hard as can be expected short of firsthand investigation (which is most unlikely to be allowed)." (Letter of Norman Hirt, *AJP*, 128:6, p. 783; see also *Psychiatric News,* June 2, 1971) [Such firsthand investigation is not very conclusive even when allowed. After a team of visiting American psychiatrists finally got permission to visit General Grigorenko, he refused to see them on the grounds that he didn't have his own interpreter, and he would not trust anyone else's. The Soviets cited this as evidence of his illness. *(Psychiatric News,* March 20, 1974)]

The documents sent by Bukovsky to The Times were translated by "The Working Group on the Internment of Dissenters in Medical Hospitals" and evaluated by forty-four psychiatrists from the Department of Psychiatry, Sheffield University. The psychiatrists described the documents in the August 1971 *British Journal of Psychiatry* and wrote a letter to *The Times* (September 16, 1971) in which they said that four of the six dissenters showed no signs or history of mental illness, and the other two had minor psychiatric problems many years earlier, quite removed from the events associated with their confinement. They recommended that the World Congress of Psychiatry consider the matter at its Mexico City meeting in November, just two months away.

The World Congress of Psychiatry

Other participants in the controversy were also looking toward the impending world congress as a forum for the issue of political misuse of psychiatry. Within the Soviet Union, the chronicle of the Medvedev case, *A Question of Madness,* shows that in June 1970 both the head of the Serbsky Institute and the Medvedevs themselves were sensitive to the possibility that Zhores Medvedev's confinement in the Kaluga mental hospital for nineteen days—amid wide protest among Soviet dissidents and coverage in the foreign press—might become an issue at the World Congress. While trying to free his brother, Roy Medvedev at one point said to Lifshits, the psychiatrist in charge:

> *I believe everything that has happened is an outrage against medicine and psychiatry. Think of the consequences and of your reputation. It will not be too difficult for us to find a way of raising the question of such actions at the International Psychiatric Congress. (Medvedev and Medvedev, 1971:85)*

At another point, he said that Snezhnevsky, the chief psychiatrist of the Ministry of Health, commented on the case: "In a year's time there is going to be an international psychiatric congress in Mexico. How do you think this is going to make our delegation look?" By the time of the World Congress, the documents sent by Bukovsky had been translated and discussed in both the psychiatric and the popular press in England. The chronicle of the confinement and later release of Zhores Medvedev had been published in English. The Soviet Human Rights Committee had appealed to the World Congress to create permanent associations in several countries to fight the use of psychiatry for repression and had called on the U. N. to create international norms for the treatment of people declared mentally ill. *(The Times,* October 23, 1971)

Only three days before the World Congress was to start, the World Federation for Mental Health passed a resolution on "misuse of psychiatric diagnosis . . . in particular—though not exclusively—against political dissent in the USSR." Only one member of the sixty-man executive board dissented. *(Psychiatric News,* January 5, 1972)

In the United States, the executive council of the American Psychiatric Association was made aware of the Canadian Psychiatric Association's resolution and was supplied with its documentation. The group also observed and recorded in its minutes the communication to the World Congress of Dr. Henri Ey condemning the use of psychiatry as an instrument of social repression. The Board of Trustees of the APA passed a resolution opposing ". . . the misuse of psychiatric facilities for the detention of persons solely on the basis of their political dissent, no matter where it occurs." However, it passed this resolution on December 9, 1971, after the World Congress had convened. (See *AJP,* Vol. 128:10, p. 1343; and *Psychiatric News,* January 5, 1972, p. 1.)

The Congress took place in Mexico City, November 28 to December 4, 1971. I. F. Stone described the events at the Congress:

> *Dr. Ramon de la Fuente, President of the Congress and President-elect of the Mexican Academy of Medicine, in his opening address said numerous documents had been received about "some places in the world" where political oppositionists were treated as mentally ill. "To keep silent about such an ignominious situation," Dr. de la Fuente said, "would weigh heavily upon our conscience." (New York Review of Books, Vol. 18, No. 2, February 10, 1972, p. 8)*

Several delegations presented resolutions. The statement of the forty-four British psychiatrists was distributed to the 7000 delegates in English, French, and Spanish. There were statements from the Soviet Human Rights Committee describing the role that Dr. Snezhnevsky, head of the Soviet delegation, had played in the Medvedev case.

> *When speakers demanded that the Congress go on record against the commitment of dissenters to mental hospitals, Dr. Snezhnevsky and the Soviet delegation at once walked out. They said that they could not discuss the matter because the Congress lacked official interpretation into Russian. (Stone, 1972:9)*

In the end, the World Congress took no action. *Psychiatric News* reported that:

> *It became clear as the week progressed that its (WPA) leaders had no desire to take an action that would have alienated the Soviet delegation and would quite likely cause them to 'walk out' and break off communications for some time to come." (January 5, 1972)*

Two months after the World Congress failed to act, I. F. Stone described both the Soviet practices and the failure of the World Congress to act. In the *New York Review of Books* (February 10, 1972) and in the *New York Times* Op. Ed. page (February 15, 1972), he reviewed the Medvedev books and described events at the World Congress. In addition, he referred to the *Report of the First U.S. Mission on Mental Health to the USSR*. This mission had visited the Soviet Union in September of 1967. It consisted of five physicians, the director of the National Committee Against Mental Illness, and the Honorable David L. Bazelon, Chief Judge of the U.S. Court of Appeals for the District of Columbia. The report of the mission, issued in February 1969, dealt mostly with the administration and delivery of mental health services. It is rather informal and nontechnical and includes many snapshots of the commissioners on their tour, outside of this or that hospital. It also contains a more scholarly Part II, "The Interface between Russian Psychiatry and the Law," written by Judge Bazelon.

Stone noted that, in commenting on the charges of Soviet misuse of psychiatry, Dr. Snezhnevsky on three occasions cited the above report as if it exonerated the Soviet Union of these charges.

> Since this report is being cited by Soviet apologists in the current contro-versy over a fundamental question which never arose during their visit, Judge Bazelon and his colleagues owe it to themselves and to the cause of justice to examine the diagnostic reports and the other documents received in England from Bukovsky and to make public their evaluation of them. The New York Review at my suggestion has asked Amnesty International in England to supply the full documentation and we will make it available to Judge Bazelon and his colleagues when it arrives. If Judge Bazelon and his colleagues reject the task of examining these records, then an ad hoc group of American Psychiatrists should do what the forty-four psychiatrists did in Britain and make their own report. (Stone, 1972:10)

In the *New York Times,* Stone added the following:

> A special obligation rests on Judge Bazelon. He was the member of the mission who visited the Serbsky Psychiatric Institute. Judge Bazelon later wrote the introduction to the English translation of the standard Soviet work on Forensic Psychiatry. . . . Neither in the report nor in the introduc-tion does he show any awareness that the Serbsky is notorious among the dissidents as a K.G.B. institution. It is clear that Judge Bazelon was treated with less than candor by his Soviet hosts. (February 15, 1972, p. 33)

While the report itself makes no mention of the use of psychiatry as a means of social control, it is not uncritical of Soviet judicial safeguards against mistakes in the judicial process. Bazelon commented:

> In practice Russian court psychiatrists seem to make decisions that are virtually unreviewable. . . . The Russians contend that judicial review is unnecessary because the psychiatrists have no motive to commit or detain a patient unjustifiably. But judicial review in this country is not premised on the belief that psychiatrists will act in bad faith. It is predicated on the belief that even the most conscientious and well-meaning psychiatrists will sometimes depart from legal and medical standards. (Bazelon, 1969: 75, 94-5)

Bazelon did visit the Serbsky Institute where he observed "the use of soldiers as guards. Such elaborate precautions, it was explained, were necessary because the Serbsky examines some of the most difficult cases in the Soviet Union." (1969:77)

Commentary It is important to point out that Bukovsky was not the first to make charges about the Soviet use of psychiatry as an instrument of social control. This practice has been described in various testimonials over the preceding years, sometimes identifying specific cases. It was also detailed by Alexander Solzhenitsyn.

The publication in the West of *The First Circle, Five Years in the Life of Ivan Denisovitch,* and *Cancer Ward* provided a background for the consideration and assessment of the charges made by Bukovsky.

Unlike previous reports that had emanated from the USSR, however, Bukovsky provided a more authoritative "documentation of the condition." He presented *The Times* with actual psychiatric dossiers, a form of evidence quite different from a novelistic narrative or an anonymous, thinly-disguised, second-hand account. Bukovsky's claim that the documents were bona fide psychiatric records presented the psychiatrists with the issue of honoring them as such and examining them against professional standards.

The Bukovsky documents were of interest to groups with different pre-occupations. Some groups were especially interested in documenting repressive practices, torture, and the stifling of political dissent. Amnesty International, for example, is concerned with psychiatric practices *only* when they are implicated in violations of human rights. Other groups were primarily concerned with the image of psychiatry and had no sustained interest in a crusade against the Soviet Union. They wanted to denounce the abuse of psychiatry in the USSR in order to affirm their own adherence to the highest ethical standards of professional practice.

In the early stage of the social problem, participants search for an effective way of presenting their claims and documenting the condition. A letter published by the *British Journal of Psychiatry* or *The Times* was a modest beginning. The World Conference of Psychiatry, however, was a forum with much more opportunity for worldwide publicity. It provided, furthermore, the possibility of confronting Soviet delegates with charges difficult to ignore, avoid, deny, or rebut. However, other goals of the World Conference, such as establishing and developing professional ties with Soviet psychiatry, interfered with its taking a clear and strong position on the charges. Eliminating the abuse of psychiatric practices was only one of their subsidiary goals, and under pressure, the Conference was unwilling to put aside its other interest.

The Ad Hoc Committee on the Use of Psychiatric
Institutions for the Commitment of
Political Dissenters

The American Psychiatric Association took note of the Stone articles almost immediately. Its Director of Public Affairs and editor of *Psychiatric News* (the APA newspaper), Robert L. Robinson, urged the medical director of the APA, Walter Barton, to reply to the Stone articles. Robinson wrote:

> *I would hate to see the NYR state in print that the authors of the report had no comment. . . . P.S. I also expect the APA will be pressured into setting up a task force to study the documents. My guess is that the pressure will come from NIMH and from a good many members. (Memo from Robinson to Barton, dated February 17, 1972)*

In early March 1972, the Board of Trustees authorized the president of the American Psychiatric Association to appoint an ad hoc committee to look into "new documentation said to be available" on the misuse of psychiatric facilities in the USSR. The Board asked that the committee submit its report at the annual meeting in May. The report of this decision in *Psychiatric News* noted that:

> *The vote and preceding debate came as a result of national publicity concerning recent charges about commitment in the Soviet Union and the failure of the World Congress of Psychiatry to act on the matter. (April 5, 1972)*

The report cited the December 9th resolution condemning the misuse of psychiatry and also noted that I. F. Stone had criticized this as an "innocuous formulation."

The APA noted in its March meeting that its December resolution was "not the consequence of the World Psychiatric Association's failure to act, but had been under study for more than one year before that meeting by several groups within the APA; namely, the Assembly and the Committee on Public Information. (*Psychiatric News*, April 5, 1972, p. 5)

The ad hoc committee was chaired by Dr. Raymond Waggoner, a past president of the APA and a member of its Board of Trustees. Other members of the committee were Dr. John Visher, Dr. Paul Chodoff, and Judge David Bazelon. Bazelon is an honorary fellow of the APA and a recipient of that organization's prized Isaac Ray award. He had been a member of the mission on mental health and a coauthor of the report mentioned earlier. This committee met twice, April 13 and April 21, 1972, and did its work quickly. They evaluated the Russian documents and recommended to the Board of Trustees the following:

1.   The President of the World Psychiatric Association be asked to circulate the APA position statement to all national societies which are members of the WPA, requesting their endorsement of the principle expressed in the APA resolution.

2.   An appropriate international organization be urged to establish a properly staffed agency to formulate internationally acceptable standards and guidelines to safeguard involuntary hospitalization from political influences as far as possible, to receive complaints from any individual or appropriate national body alleging the enforced use of psychiatric facilities for political purposes, and to make investigations of such complaints. (AJP, 129:4, p. 507)

All members of the ad hoc committee approved this report and the Board of Trustees endorsed their recommendation in their April meeting.

Ad Hoc Committee to Study Conflicts Inherent in the Therapeutic and Institutional Roles of Psychiatry

One member of the committee, Judge David Bazelon, felt that the potential for coercive use of psychiatry was not confined to the Soviet Union, and that there was really very little that professional groups in the United States could do about political repression inside the Soviet Union. In April 1972 he discussed the work of the committee with Eleanor Glass, a recent Yale Law School graduate, who was clerking in the judge's chambers. She reported:

He didn't know whether it was worth really trying to make a point or to just let it slide with some wishy-washy statement about the Russians. . . . And he said I'll give you the documents and you think about it. If you would like to get involved in this, I'll get involved. If you'd like to do the work. . . .I mean, the judge felt strongly about the issue, but his time is already so over-committed. . . . I discussed it with George (her husband, a psychiatrist serving in the Navy and displeased with his work there) and he got very interested in it. Then we were at a cocktail party and George got the judge in a corner and talked about it and they both got very excited about it. . . . So, basically George and I agreed that we would write out a first draft of the statement and the judge would append this to any kind of report that the committee as a whole was going to submit. (Interview with Eleanor Glass, September 4, 1974, pp. 3-4)

This statement, nine typewritten pages, was appended to the one-and-one-half-page report of the ad hoc committee. It argued that the potential for abuse of psychiatry was not confined to the Soviet Union, nor was it limited to actions taken against a handful of highly visible political activists. Whenever psychiatrists abandon their role as the ally of the patient, the patient's agent in the medical treatment of mental illness, psychiatry has been abused.

> *When the psychiatrist's posture toward a patient is altered, however, the underpinnings of our trust vanish. Psychiatrists have applied [their] knowledge at the request of a variety of public and social institutions; communities, the military, political, judicial and penal institutions to name a few. The task set for them by these institutions is to diagnostically label and treat individuals for institutional purposes—generally to retain the status quo and suppress deviance which is detrimental to the institution. It is both inaccurate and dangerous for us to continue to consider the use of psychiatric methodology in these settings to be within the traditional definition of psychiatry—"the medical treatment of mental illness." (Bazelon, 1972, pp. 5-6)*

The judge suggested that psychiatrists must understand and recognize conflict situations as such, make these conflicts known to their patients, and encourage third-party review of their most critical decisions. While he made no very specific or concrete suggestions, he urged the APA not to hide behind a smoke screen of protestations of good faith and pretend that such situations do not exist and to actively identify and bring to light those situations where institutional interests conflict with and undermine the doctor-patient relationship:

> *The profession must ask itself whether it wants to assume both the janitorial function, and responsibility, of helping to sweep some of society's most troublesome problems under the rug. . . . What is . . . urgently needed is for the psychiatric profession to stop sweeping its own problems under the rug and to conduct an in-depth inquiry into the use of psychiatric discipline in the institutions of our own society. (1972, p. 9)*

In response to this report, which was cosigned by Raymond Waggoner, chairman of the ad hoc committee, the Board of Trustees in May extended the life of the ad hoc committee for one year in order to explore the issues raised by Judge Bazelon's statement. The committee was authorized to seek private funds in order to conduct research. *Psychiatric News* (July 5, 1972) publicized the activities of the committee and invited interested parties to communicate with the committee, especially if they had "documentary evidence of the improper use of psychiatric facilities and conflicts of interest." The members met for the first time on May 17, 1972 to consider its new mandate. They expanded the membership of the committee by inviting Harold Visotsky and Lloyd Baccus, both psychiatrists, to become members, and they appointed

Eleanor Glass as secretary. The members then discussed in general terms what their research should demonstrate. Bazelon, through his friend Douglas Bond, President of the W. T. Grant Foundation, had informal assurances that that organization would fund the research, perhaps $50,000 to $80,000. The committee obtained a grant of $6,000 to design the research and select their personnel.

Commentary   The arena in which this social problem was conducted changed from the World Conference on Psychiatry to the committee structure of the American Psychiatric Association. Perhaps there were continuing activities in other countries or groups as well. The publications of I. F. Stone, his "call to set the record straight," and letters to the editor of *Psychiatric News* help us understand how interest in this problem was sustained and why the APA responded quickly.

The ad hoc committee, after examining the documents, agreed that a problem existed and issued a statement saying that "something should be done." A small committee issued a public statement calling for someone to do something. At this point, David Bazelon entered the social problems process. He began to shift the nature of the claims and to focus the issue, not only on the USSR, but on the U.S. Bazelon, chief judge of the U.S. Court of Appeals in Washington, D.C., was a prominent member of an already prominent profession and respected as a legal scholar whose opinions and writings are still considered among the finest in jurisprudence. In addition, he had a long and active interest in psychiatry and its relation to the law. He authored the controversial Durham Rule, which was established as the standard for judging the adequacy of insanity as a defense in criminal proceedings. Bazelon received the Isaac Ray Award from the American Psychiatric Association for service to psychiatry, was elected President of the American Ortho-Psychiatric Association, appointed to numerous blue-ribbon panels on mental health problems, and participated in the first U.S. Mission on Mental Health to the USSR. We enumerate Judge Bazelon's credentials to underline the political significance of the report he appended to the report of the Ad Hoc Committee on the Misuse of Psychiatry.

Bazelon did more than say, "Let's look at the same thing in our country before we denounce what others are doing." He suggested, first of all, that the misuse of psychiatry involved more than the issue of locking up a few dozen prominent political dissidents or troublemakers. He argued that psychiatrists are involved in a wide range of relationships. Some are limited to the privacy of the patient's communications with his doctor; others, however, are more public in the sense that third parties also have relationships with the psychiatrist. Bazelon considerably enlarged the scope of "the condition" beyond the misuse of psychiatry to various relationships in which psychiatrists are confronted with conflicts of interest. Furthermore, the term "conflict of interest" linked Bazelon's analysis to situations confronted by professionals and officials in other institutional settings. That is, the term is applied to relationships in which the impartiality of any official might be questioned or impugned. When Bazelon called for an examination of the misuse of psychiatry in the U.S., he was also changing and enlarging the condition to be examined and, by implication, the definition of the problem.

Selecting a Research Team

By the July 8, 1972 meeting the search for a research staff was underway. The committee had voted to change its name to the Ad Hoc Committee to Study Conflicts Inherent in the Therapeutic and Institutional Role of Psychiatry. The group agreed that its research should show whether conflicts of interest existed, whether they were more widespread than isolated anecdotes might suggest, whether the rights of many individuals were being violated, and whether medical needs of institutionalized patients were frequently sacrificed to facilitate institutional needs. The committee quickly agreed that the researchers should be sociologists:

The committee knew it had to be sociologists looking at this. (Why did it have to be sociologists?) Well, I think everyone agreed that psychiatrists were much too close to it. We wanted an objective look at patient-doctor relationships. We wanted to look at the various factors acting on the doctor as a decision-maker. There had to be a methodology to our research, someone who could design for us a way to study this issue and I think that was even more up front in our thinking. We didn't know how to study this issue and we had to hire someone who knows how to look at problems, problems of society, and to us that meant a sociologist. (Did you have any sense that sociologists are very frequently anti-psychiatry?)

Yes, I did. I think they did too. . . . It was only after I went to New Orleans (to attend the American Sociological Association convention) that I found this out, that sociologists themselves who made it their profession to study psychiatry have radically different views of psychiatry and what psychiatry is and should be doing in society. . . . I was not able to convey to them (the committee) a real understanding of, you know, what this split in sociology was, because I'm not sure I understood it myself. And it would take a great deal of reading to keep that under your belt. (Nobody else on the committee had any knowledge. . . .) Nobody else. (And yet, they wanted to hire a sociologist?) Oh, yes. (Interview with E. Glass, September 1974, pp. 18-21)

During the summer of 1972 the committee searched for a sociologist to command the research team. Committee members were supposed to go back to their home universities, call up the chairman of the sociology department, and ask who might be interested in the topic. That suggestion produced no results at all. Eleanor Glass did most of the legwork of the committee. By the July 8th meeting she had talked with about a dozen sociologists and generated a list of people to contact. She telephoned prominent people in sociology and asked them if they might be interested or if they could recommend someone who was. These included Orville Brim, David Mechanic, Erving Goffman, Thomas Scheff, Eliot Freidson, and Judith Lorber.

> *But the big wheels were not interested in us, you know. They didn't have the time. (You asked them?) Yes . . . we wanted somebody that could give us at least a half-time commitment. We didn't want a big cheese at a university who was going to farm this out to graduate students. . . . From the beginning it was clear among the committee members that we wanted somebody who was going to give us a lot of time, somebody the committee could work with and count on. (Interview with E. Glass, September 1974, p. 22)*

Many of the people who were unwilling to devote so much time to the project recommended others who might be prepared to do so. One person recommended by a number of the "big cheeses," Arlene Daniels, met with a committee member, John Visher, in August. He wrote to Waggonner, the chairman of the committee, in late August:

> *I have developed a new and presumably healthy awareness of the complexities of the issues which our committee is attempting to address. . . . There are many fascinating side issues with political and other implications which would appear to be potentially very serious. For example, an inquiry into military psychiatry sponsored by the APA could well blow the lid off, revealing some rather messy issues. (Visher to Waggoner, August 24, 1972)*

Several weeks later the Executive Committee of the APA met and approved the change in name of the committee, authorized $2,000 for their use in hiring a research staff, but also "urged constraint in the focus of the mission." (*AJP,* 130:10, p. 1181) in a memo to Waggoner, Walter Barton, the medical director, said:

> *The Executive Committee was also concerned that you had broadened the charge of the ad hoc committee far beyond the original intent and seemed to be continually broadening it. They hoped that you would focus on a manageable topic as you seemed to be doing at your last meeting. (September 15, 1972)*

The ad hoc committee had not been very specific about what it wanted to do. The nine-page statement by Bazelon was, four months later, still the most current statement of its mandate. It was sent to those who expressed interest in submitting plans for the research. Even a year later it was being circulated as a current description of the problem. Committee members believed that they could not examine conflicts of interest without raising larger questions about the nature of psychiatry. Some felt that if they attempted to specify the accepted medical standards in psychiatry from which a doctor might deviate, it was:

> . . . a foot in the door for the question, what is psychiatry? What do they know? What do they do? Why do they have the power that they have? Are they really helping people, or not? (Interview with E. Glass, September 1974, p. 9)

The one-year mandate suggested that the issues were so big that the most the committee could do was to gather materials to properly raise these questions, not propose solutions and give answers. The policy implications were never seriously discussed or debated.

> (Now, did people discuss at this time [Summer 1972] what they thought ought to be done about the conflicts of interest?) No. (Policy?) Never. (Change?) No. (Legislation?) No. The most that was said was that the psychologists had just come out with some kind of code of ethics, parts of which governed some sort of conflict situations. It was just a tremendously exciting idea for everybody to think what the APA would do if it was really presented with a convincing case. The most that was formulated was that in some way the profession would try to point in a direction to which some of the conflicts could be resolved, either in training or in the military. They said that if a psychiatrist could say, "Hey, look, the APA is telling me I can't do this. I can't change my diagnosis that I believe in," then it would give the psychiatrist a leg to stand on in fighting his military bosses. (Interview with E. Glass, September 1974, pp. 33-34)

Even Judge Bazelon, whose statement led to the extension of the ad hoc committee, had no clear plans in mind, nor was he committed to crusading for change. In answer to a question concerning the advisability of a strategy linking the issue of conflicts of interest to a reevaluation of psychiatry as a whole, he replied:

> What strategy? We had no special strategy. We weren't plotting to get one point of view adopted. We just wanted to open the area up, air the issues. Then who knows what we would have wanted to recommend? (Interview with David Bazelon, September 1974)

The committee held a competition to choose a research team. On September 15-16, 1972 six such groups presented their research proposals and credentials to the committee in Washington. Each team had expressed interest and sent in a written proposal in advance. Three were considered seriously. Two teams were invited to submit further proposals in writing. One team, headed by Nevit Sanford who was from the Wright Institute, impressed the committee with a polished written document, but:

> *It was clear he wasn't going to give it much time. It was going to be a factory job. The involvement of the committee was going to be absolutely minimal in his project. He would get a couple of good theses out of it for the graduate students. They weren't offering us one solid name. It was going to be one 10 percent or 30 percent and two 50 percent people. (Interview with E. Glass, September 1974, p. 29)*

A second team was headed by Arlene Daniels of Scientific Analysis Corporation. Glass had contacted her during the summer, and they had discussed the project in New Orleans at the sociology convention. She invited Robert Weiss to join her application as a methodological consultant. Their presentation stressed the work that Daniels had already done on conflicts of interest in military psychiatry, an area in which she had several recent publications. She said that she had much data relevant to the ad hoc committee's interest in 100 interviews collected over the last several years. She would analyze these for the committee. In addition, a literature review would identify which areas were relatively well documented and which were not. She also offered to design feasibility studies in several areas, arguing that within the time and financial strictures of the committee, it would be unwise and a waste of time and money to attempt the major studies that the committee seemed to require in order to answer its questions and to meet its own objectives.

The minutes of the meetings of September 15-16 reveal that the committee felt that Daniels and Weiss were both extremely competent and familiar with the area. The members also felt the data that Daniels was prepared to put at the committee's disposal were invaluable:

> *Her data is [sic] basically of sufficient depth and quality that would be difficult to duplicate. It is the product of many years of work from extensive in-depth interviews. This is the type of data that we will eventually want in whatever settings we choose, and she posed a serious question as to whether the committee could afford or would get such sophisticated data on which to build an analysis of specific bureaucratic settings. (Ad Hoc Committee Minutes, September 15-16, p. 5)*

Dr. Daniels' "strong personality" and her known hostility to some psychiatric practices were discussed, but her expertise and knowledge of the area were seen as offsetting factors. Also, while Daniels had said she would devote up to fifty percent of her time to the project, the committee was not altogether pleased that she would be bringing so much of her own data and expertise with her:

She was going to do it pretty much full time, but it was that the committee would lose control. This was going to be her project. We felt, and it was in part geographic, that there was really no role the committee could perceive for itself in her project other than she would report to us what she had found. The committee really would have no control over her, other than to veto what she said. (Interview with E. Glass, September 1974, pp. 30-31)

The final research team, the one that in the end was chosen, consisted of Donald Light, Joseph Perpich, Franklin Chu, and Sharland Trotter. Light was a sociologist from Princeton; Perpich was a research psychiatrist with the National Institute for Mental Health (NIMH) and later with the Institute of Medicine; Chu and Trotter were authors of a Nader report on community mental health facilities.

Chu and Trotter were already acquainted with Judge Bazelon. In the course of their work on community psychiatry, they had often talked with him about their ideas. The judge liked them, thought they were bright, and that they would be good staff or legpersons for the research of the ad hoc committee. In August they talked with Eleanor Glass about the proposed research, said they were interested, and suggested that Joseph Perpich, a friend of theirs, might also be interested. He was. Each of them drafted a proposal to the ad hoc committee. These people were willing to work as a team. But Glass told them:

Well, you've got to have a sociologist. You've got to have somebody that can give you a methodology and really control you. You would be the legpeople, but you're never going to get through the (ad hoc) committee. I expressed this to the judge and he said, "Well, can't you find a sociologist for them?" (September 1974, pp. 26-27)

She contacted Light, whose name had been given to her by several sources, most recently by a psychiatrist who had been interviewed by Light in a study he conducted of psychiatric residency. Light was interested, said he could devote half of his time to the project, and came down to meet Perpich, Chu, and Trotter. They got along well and had similar ideas about the research. Light was added to the team. (The three had previously vetoed another sociologist whom they didn't like.)

Light's research proposal seemed almost designed to assuage the fears of the committee's objections to Daniels and Sanford. It conformed to the committee's growing desire to work closely with and exercise control over its staff. Light hoped that the committee would work closely with him, introduce him to people, and help guide him to the relevant literature. He proposed research in institutional settings and offered a list of such institutions, adding, "This, however, is a tentative list, and we are happy to discuss changes or additions to it." (Light proposal, page 3) He pointed out that being located in the East (three members of the team lived in Washington) they would have easy access to the committee and vice versa. Finally, Light requested office space at APA headquarters "to reduce administrative burdens on us and to facilitate communication with members of the APA who can help us on the project." (Light proposal, p. 8) Light proposed a computerized search of the literature and then fieldwork and in-depth interviews in institutions that exhibited a wide range of conflicts of interests—those resolved in favor of the patients as well as those resolved in favor of the institutions. There was some concern about the diffuse relationship between Light and the rest of the committee. But at the close of the September 15-16 meeting, the committee favored the Light-Perpich-Chu-Trotter team. As Eleanor Glass described it:

Light tuned in exactly to what the committee saw as its role, and the committee wanted a strong role for itself. They [the research team] were the tools of the committee. (September 1974, p. 32)

The committee requested both Daniels and Light to submit further written proposals before October 14th. After reading the proposals, the committee chose Light. The research was to begin in January 1973 and preparations were made to get the project underway. In November the $80,000 grant came through from the Grant Foundation. *Psychiatric News* carried the following announcement to its 20,000 subscribers:

Two sessions at the Honolulu meetings (the annual committee in May) will be held in conjunction with research APA is undertaking on professional and political conflicts in psychiatric work. Initiated by the Ad Hoc Committee to Study Conflicts Inherent in the Therapeutic and Institutional Role of Psychiatry, the research will focus on psychiatrists who work for institutions, such as state hospitals, prisons and private industry, and who experience conflicting pressures in their work to abandon their role as the patients' agent and to use their skills to serve institutional purposes. (December 20, 1972)

The preliminary program of the annual meetings scheduled a plenary session in which members of the committee and the research team would present their preliminary findings.

Commentary In this section, we have a clear example of how sociologists may be participants, rather than analysts, in the development of a social problem. Faced with the task of appointing a research team, the ad hoc committee sought the services of sociologists. The members thought the issues were sociological and that sociologists have the specialized training, research experience, and appropriate theoretical knowledge to investigate the problem and document the conditions. They apparently did not consider other categories of researchers, such as psychologists, political scientists, or anthropologists, and assumed that this was the kind of issue that called for sociological research.

The committee's search for a research team and the difficulties encountered in locating an appropriate principal investigator underline another aspect of documenting social conditions. Although the members conceived the problem to be within the specialized field of medical sociology, they were unable to locate sociologists of sufficient stature who had recognized expertise in their topic. Their difficulty exemplifies the problematic features of the documentation of claims. Some claims do not lend themselves easily to documentation. The kinds of data that might be produced and, when produced, acknowledged as relevant to the claims being made are not self-evident. Thus, while the committee appeared to be committed to social science research as the proper procedure for the investigation of the problem, the existing organization of research in medical sociology did not provide them with a category of researcher that would generate a list of possible candidates to do the job.

The Disbanding of the Committee

During the meeting of September 16, when the Light team seemed to have a strong edge over the Daniels team, Paul Chodoff remarked to Chairman Waggoner, "Chu and Trotter are going to be very controversial, and you had better check it out with the executive committee." (Interview with E. Glass, 1974, p. 35) Waggoner contacted some trustees on the executive committee. The response was strongly negative. Chu and Trotter had recently circulated a preliminary draft of their report on community mental health centers. While few of the executive committee members had seen or read it, they reacted to rumors that it was biased against psychiatry, that some persons had claimed to be misquoted in it, and that the report damaged the psychiatric lobby on Capitol Hill. A special joint meeting of the ad hoc committee with the executive committee was scheduled for October 14, 1972. In the meantime, Glass had written to Light about the controversy and he responded by outlining an interviewing procedure that would be used to control, compensate and remove any possible bias in the two junior interviewers. He also expressed confidence in their abilities.

The joint meeting took place as scheduled, and two issues were discussed. The first concerned the objectivity of Chu and Trotter. The executive committee asked why two people with known biases against psychiatry had been hired. With 200 million people in the country, wasn't there anyone else who could do this work? The committee members responded that they had interviewed five or six teams, their decision had not been made hastily, and they had picked the best group that had the time to devote to the research.

In addition, a certain theme was introduced at this meeting that continued to reappear throughout the controversy and its aftermath. In the week before the meeting there had been a lot of discussion among members of the APA executives:

> They viewed it as a Bazelon plot. And I think there was other gossip that this whole thing blew up because Dave wanted to give these two kids a job; that he had just railroaded the decision through and he had the committee in the palm of his hand; that they were his puppets.... People called Visotsky and said, "How could you get involved in this? What has Dave done to you?" What they finally came up with was this cliche that the judge prefers the adversary system and they prefer the scientific system. (Interview with E. Glass, September 1974, p. 43)

Judd Marmor, in particular, attacked the "adversary approach" in the meeting:

> Dr. Marmor asked that the executive committee be objective and approach the matter without preconceptions, that the adversary system called for a lawyer's brief that sets forth the arguments in favor of a proposition. This was not the approach that psychiatry wished to use. A truly objective approach to the problem is desired where one is not trying to prove a preconception.... The method of science is to try to compensate for bias, and while the adversary system may be appropriate in court, it's not appropriate in psychiatry. (Minutes of the joint meeting, October 14, 1972, p. 3)

Beginning in January and continuing throughout the coverage of the committee controversy, *Psychiatric News* made constant references to the "adversary method of the committee." At one point it reported:

> The trustees expressed some concern that the committee seemed to be tending toward an "adversary" approach in the study, entailing employment of investigators with predetermined biases, rather than an objective scholarly approach. (January 3, 1973)

In another article (August 15, 1973) the paper refers to the "by then obvious adversary bias" that emerged in the committee in the fall of 1972. Rebutting this reference, Visher, Visotsky, and Chairman Waggoner wrote a letter to the editor:

The committee itself never saw the project as having any relationship to the adversary process mentioned in **Psychiatric News,** *nor were there any plans to use adversary methods in the collection of objective data. Neither the research proposal, nor the Light team, nor any minutes of the Ad Hoc Committee's meetings contain references to adversary methods, nor is there any definition of how adversary methods might play any role in research as opposed to their function in judicial proceedings. (***Psychiatric News,** *November 21, 1973)*

The October 14, 1972 meeting of the Executive Committee ended with a resolution approving the research in principle, but urging care in the choice of staff and personnel. Four days later, on October 18, 1972, Walter Barton, the APA medical director, wrote to Waggoner, saying there would be a meeting on November 4th "at which time we will meet with Dr. Light and hopefully Dr. Perpich and discuss the possibility of the use of graduate students in place of Chu and Trotter." However, this was not really possible.

It was theoretically possible for me to let Chu and Trotter go and get some other people. But that ignored the human realities. Joe (Perpich) said he would quit without the other two. So that was that. (Interview with Donald Light, July 27, 1974)

On November 4th, the committee thought the issue was finally settled. The staff prepared to begin the research in January. At the December 8th meeting of the Board of Trustees, the issue became deadlocked. While the funds had come through from the Grant Foundation, Walter Barton refused to sign the contract because it specifically referred to Chu and Trotter. This meant that the funds could not be properly transferred from the foundation to the APA and, in effect, it froze the project. The Board asked Waggoner, chairman of the ad hoc committee (and a member of the board), to reconsider the choice of personnel.

Waggoner told the trustees that he could not continue as chairman of the committee unless the board trusted his judgment about who should be hired to conduct the study's research. One trustee moved that the board express confidence in the work of the committee, but instruct it not to employ Chu and Trotter. Waggoner warned that if this motion passed, he would resign as committee chairman. The motion was carried by a vote of 9 to 6, and as promised, Waggoner quit. . . . At lunch an APA vice president indicated to Waggoner that he would try to get the vote rescinded so that Waggoner could continue as chairman, if Waggoner promised to attempt to convince the ad hoc committee not to use Chu and Trotter. Waggoner so promised and agreed to resign if he could not get the committee to reconsider. On that basis, the morning's motion was unanimously rescinded. (Miller, 1973, p. 247)

The board then set up a three-person subcommittee to meet with the ad hoc committee on December 16, 1972. Only one member of this subcommittee, Melvin Sabshin, attended. He told the committee that the Board of Trustees would probably disband the committee if Chu and Trotter were kept. After a long debate, the ad hoc committee voted to ask the Board of Trustees to reconsider its position.

Finally, in early February, 1973, the Board of Trustees met and again considered the question of the ad hoc committee. Waggoner, a member of the Board of Trustees, was in attendance. In addition, Visotsky appeared by invitation to defend the position of the committee. In the meantime, several other issues had arisen to join the controversies over the adversary process and the question of Chu and Trotter. The quality of the research proposal and the reputation and competence of the two principal researchers, Light and Perpich, had become an issue. A December 22nd letter from Douglas Bond of the funding agency remarked "Perpich has hardly established himself as an investigator. . .Light is hardly in a better category." The letter seemed to negate all the work the committee had done during the previous summer and fall. In the February meeting of the Board, Dr. Busse:

. . . stated in careful and very tactful terms that he was somewhat disturbed at the selection of this team in that members of his faculty at Duke did not know of Dr. Light, nor did he ever see a CV on Dr. Perpich. . . . He stated that Dr. Light talked with him, but to this date he had not been able to obtain from Dr. Light any publications or significant research that would enlighten him as to the competence of Dr. Light. Dr. Milton Greenblatt felt that the research design in this project was extremely poor and did not meet the barest essentials of a research protocol. . . . The plan of study was criticized specifically again by Dr. Robert Felix, a past president of the APA and a former director of the National Institute of Mental Health. Dr. Felix stated that, were this presented to a study committee of the National Institute of Mental Health, it would be rejected . . . I must point out that I sat next to Bob Felix. I asked him if he had read the full report. He stated, "No," that he had heard about it. . . . It was apparent to me, throughout the comments that almost all of the people had not read all of the material presented by the committee. (Minutes, p. 2)

Following this debate, the Board of Trustees voted to disband the ad hoc committee to Study Conflicts Inherent in the Therapeutic and Institutional

Roles of Psychiatry and requested the Council on Research and Development to appoint a task force to consider the whole matter. In a letter dated February 23, 1973, Walter Barton informed Sidney Malitz, the Chairman of the APA Council on Research and Development, of the decision to disband the committee and turn the project over to Malitz. He ends his letter:

If you have any questions, do call Dr. Work as you'll want to get a firm grip on the tail of this tiger.

This February meeting was apparently very volatile. At one point the question was asked:

"Isn't it true that Judge Bazelon dictated a letter for your [Waggoner's] signature, appointing Dr. Thomas Szasz as a senior consultant and senior final editor of the report?". . . I said that such statements represented the mood, the level of acceptance of rumor, rather than fact . . . facts which were available in the minutes of our committee . . . and were prejudiced to a fair and objective evaluation. Many of the Board Members shouted agreement, and withdrew the question. (Minutes, p.5)

In addition, Harold Visotsky noted that:

This is the first time in my experience that there was not a transcript made of the meeting, even though this was an official part of the Board of Trustee's meeting. I would assume that this was somewhat of a departure from the usual Board of Trustees' meeting procedures, since I have always seen recording equipment at previous meetings.

On this same point in a letter from Visotsky to Waggoner, Visotsky described an incident at a later meeting.

And aside from that Perry forgot that a recording of that meeting was not made, and said, "Let's review the tapes of that meeting." It brought some laughter, since that was a departure from their usual procedures in not taping that meeting. I will go through this at greater length when I see you. (May 22, 1973)

Thomas Szasz did not meet with the committee, nor was he a consultant of the committee. He was, however, asked to act as one of several consultants to the committee and either declined or ignored the request. An exchange of letters between Perry Tarkington and Raymond Waggoner in the summer of 1972, when the committee was formulating its ideas and considering research teams, shows the following:

I will leave it to your judgment as to whether or not Poussaint and/or Szasz should be invited to meet one or more times with the committee. (Tarkington to Waggoner, August 2, 1972)

I think it would be wise to ask Dr. Poussaint and Dr. Szasz to meet both days of the meetings. . . . If we do this we will avoid criticism of our action from the groups that these two men would represent and too, they might have an input which would be quite valuable. (Waggoner to Tarkington, August 10, 1972)

I completely agree with your decision to ask Poussaint and Szasz. (Tarkington to Waggoner, August 15, 1972)

It was, however, Tarkington himself who asked whether Szasz was to be the final senior editor of the project.

Aftermath of Disbanding the Committee

The Council on Research and Development to which the project was assigned began to search for a team to conduct the research for the APA. None of the members of the ad hoc committee were invited to participate in the new effort, nor were any of them consulted in either the definition of the project or in the choice of personnel. Members of the disbanded committee did not, however, forget the project or abandon their efforts to pursue the research. A memo dated March 13, 1973 from four committee members, Bazelon, Visher, Visotsky, and Waggoner, requested John Hogness, President of the Institute of Medicine at the National Academy of Science, to consider taking up the project. They sent him a seven-page history of the committee to which they appended the Bazelon statement of April 1972. The research team of Light, Perpich, Chu, and Trotter disbanded. Perpich took a job at the Institute of Medicine; Chu left to attend law school.

In the spring and summer of 1973 Judge Bazelon began publicizing the history of the committee in speeches and in published articles. The speeches include the following:

May 1973:   The third annual Helen Ross Lecture at the Institute for Psychoanalysis in Chicago

June 1973:   Meeting of the Southern California Psychiatric Society

October 1973:   Joint meeting of the Cleveland Bar Association and the Cleveland Psychiatry Society

October 1973:   The American Psychiatric Association Divisional meeting in Williamsburg, Virginia

January 1974:   Conference on Mental Health and the Law, Catholic University

May 1974:   Isaac Ray Symposium, Butler Hospital, Providence, Rhode Island

May 1974:   American Psychiatric Association, Annual Meeting

In connection with these speeches, he published articles in the *Washington Post* (June 24, 1973), the *Los Angeles Times* (July 1, 1974), and *Scientific American* (June 1974). In these speeches and articles the judge not only criticized the APA action on the ad hoc committee, but also reflected on his long contact with psychiatrists as expert witnesses before the law and through his participation in numerous professional activities in the field of mental health. He included some rather general speculations on the development of the profession and the unwillingness of a profession to police itself. He described the progress of the committee as follows:

> *As I read these case studies from the USSR, however, I was impressed to realize how, in many analogous situations in this country, I had occasion to find psychiatrists making decisions for motives and under pressures from outside their professional role. Needless to say, I found the leadership of the profession in America not nearly as eager to investigate such conflicts in their own ranks as they were to look into evidence of malpractice in the USSR. To make a not very pleasant story short, when our ad hoc committee turned its attention to the American scene, at first with official approval, its charter was soon revoked. (Bazelon, 1974:22)*

> *The APA trustees extended the life of our committee for a year so that we could study whether the conflicts in this country were in seed or in bloom. But after eight months of developing a research project, we were suddenly discharged under a barrage of ad hominem criticism. (Los Angeles Times, July 1, 1974, and Washington Post, June 24, 1973)*

In *Scientific American,* the judge did not begin with the history of the ad hoc committee, but with a review of psychiatrists' willingness to allow others to examine their conclusions in the courtroom:

> *One might hope that psychiatrists would open up their reservoirs of knowledge in the courtroom. Unfortunately, in my experience, they try to limit their testimony to conclusory statements couched in psychiatric terminology. Thereafter they take shelter in a defensive resistance to questions about the facts that are or ought to be in their possession. They thus refuse to submit their opinions to the scrutiny that the adversary process demands. . . . What psychiatrists have not understood is that conclusory labels are no substitute in judicial proceedings for facts derived from disciplined investigation. . . .*

The sterility *of the profession's response to* Durham *[the Durham decision], I now conclude, was due to the fact that its observance was bound to make the psychiatrist's task in the courtroom much more demanding than before. . . . In the end, after 18 years, I favored the abandonment of the Durham rule because in practice it had failed to take the issue of criminal responsibility away from the experts. Psychiatrists continued to testify to the naked conclusions, instead of providing information about the accused so that the jury could render the ultimate moral judgment about blameworthiness. (1974:18-21)*

The judge reviewed the Jenkens case of 1962, where the American Psychiatric Association filed a brief saying that *psychologists* should not be allowed to testify as to mental condition because they lacked the medical training of the psychiatrist. The judge comments that they

. . . overlook the fact that the problem of criminal responsibility is not the exclusive terrain of psychiatry. I wrote the opinion for our court rejecting such guild mentality. (1974:22)

In yet another case in which the court held that "adequacy of treatment is reviewable in court. . . ."

The American Psychiatric Association responded . . . with an adamant statement of what I must call professional mystique: "The definition of treatment and the appraisal of its adequacy are matters for medical determination."

What is disturbing about these situations is not that they impute venality or frailty to merely human practitioners, nor that conflicting societal interests can dictate different and not necessarily the best medical results. It is, rather, that the psychiatric profession should resist facing these conflicts in the open. Serious legal challenges have been needed to surface its hidden agenda. (1974:22)

One response to the judge's criticism came from the Medical Director of the APA, Walter Barton. In a letter to the editor of the Washington Post, he wrote:

What really irks the judge, we venture, is that we are unwilling to do it his way. He is an ardent believer in the adversary system as a means of arriving at truth. We are not. At the moment we are engaged in exploring with various universities the possibility of undertaking such a study, using objective scholars, rather than biased advocates. (July 13, 1973)

A second letter to the editor responding to Judge Bazelon's remarks appeared on the same page. Paul Chodoff, another member of the ad hoc committee, wrote:

> *The Board's real intention regarding the proposed study could have been ascertained by complying with the proposal of the trustees that Chu and Trotter be replaced by less controversial investigators. I regret that this was not done and a very important effort at self-scrutiny by the profession of psychiatry foundered in a clash of personalities.*

In another letter to the editor, this time in *Science,* Chodoff commented:

> *The demise of the committee and its projected research project is regrettable. This result, however, can be attributed more to a power conflict among strong-minded men on both sides, than to a defensive need in the psychiatric establishment to keep its skeletons from being rattled. (October 5, 1973, p. 9)*

On March 20, 1974 *Psychiatric News* carried an announcement that the Institute of Society, Ethics, and Life Sciences at Hastings-on-Hudson, New York would do a two-and-a-half-year study of the role of psychiatrists in society. Dr. Alfred Freedman, the president of the Association:

> *. . . noted that this study probably marks the first time that a major profession in American Life has undertaken on its own initiative to open itself to a comprehensive assessment by impartial scholars.*

Dr. Harold Visotsky, a vice president of the APA and a former member of the ad hoc committee, reported that the codirectors of the study would be Dr. William Gaylin and Dr. Robert Michels, the former, president of the Institute, the later, a professor of psychiatry at Cornell. He said:

> *The fact that the codirectors are psychiatrists really doesn't matter. (Psychiatric News, October 5, 1974)*

In August 1974 the funding of that study had not yet been arranged. Dr. Gaylin commented in a personal communication that he considered it "less than 50-50" whether the research would ever get funded.

Commentary   In this phase of the definitional process, the claims took new form. When the Board of Trustees disbanded the committee, Judge Bazelon leveled new charges, this time questioning the good faith and integrity of organized psychiatry. His documentation of the basis of this claim included the activities of the APA leadership in the committee controversy, but he went beyond those events and reviewed the history of the profession's response to court rulings relating to psychiatric practice. He argued first that the APA had sabotaged the Durham rule by refusing to reveal the basis of psychiatric diagnostic decisions, citing cases in which gross misrepresentation and secrecy were involved. Second, he outlined what he thought were the self-serving actions of the psychiatric profession. Examined with reference to the problem posed by Bukovsky's revelations about the misuse of psychiatry in the USSR, Bazelon's new claims gave a dramatic new direction to the definitional process.

Although Judge Bazelon was criticized and vilified for his new charges in published letters to the editor of the APA journal, the profession also moved to bring him back into the fold. In May 1975, the APA awarded Bazelon its distinguished service award for his work in the interest of psychiatry. Perhaps such awards atone for past sins of the association as well as honor, excellence, and service.

CONCLUDING REMARKS

Overall, these materials contrast sharply with most of the literature on problems in medical and psychiatric sociology. Such accounts begin to tell us something about the nature of the activities that constitute and give rise to claims-making. Typically, sociologists have not investigated the internal workings of such organizations as Amnesty International, The World Conference of Psychiatry, The American Psychiatric Association and their committee structures, where claims-making activities often emerge. Medical and psychiatric sociology have studied doctor-patient relationships, but not the organizations that negotiate the licensing arrangements and provide the backdrop for those relationships.

Our perspective led us to examine data which has always been thought relevant (see Becker, 1962, Bucher and Strauss, 1961, and Freidson, 1970) but which has not attracted systematic attention from researchers.

Our greatest departure from traditional sociological methods is the deemphasis of a traditionally conceived unit of analysis and the shifting of attention from one issue to another. The data document the development of claims and issues as they are defined, redefined, and passed from one set of participants to another; this thread of continuity leads to and through a variety of institutions and casts of characters. In addition, the focus of the data changes as new participants enter the claims-making activity, redefine the problem, and shift the focus of the activity. For example, the initial concern with abuses of psychiatry in the Soviet Union was transformed into a concern with such activities in the United States, and then further transformed into matters of good faith and integrity within the American Psychiatric Association. The unit of analysis of these data is the historical thread of continuity that resides in the interaction of participants in the unfolding and development of "the problem."

Social problem researchers are at no point required to make independent assessments of the claims-making activities they investigate. They need not decide if psychiatry is, in fact, used to repress dissidents in the USSR, if conflicts of interest are characteristic of American psychiatry, or to decide if the APA is a selfish, paranoid, and self-perpetuating oligarchy that disregards the "public interest." The researchers ask how the participants come to make these statements, what they take to be evidence of the conditions and to whom they direct their claims. Had the research proposal of Light and his associates been approved and implemented, we would have had an opportunity to examine what *this* group of participants took to be evidence of the condition and how others responded to their documentation.

These materials raise other questions. We have said that they constitute the data for the sociology of social problems, but in what way would an *analysis* of the social problem differ from this account? That is, we have already organized and reduced that documentary material to some extent. Might this not then be called an analysis of the social problem, and if so, which social problem does it analyze?

The answer in part may be that the activities described touch on a number of different social problems; that is, on a sequence of different social conditions that become the objects of definition, claims, and controversy. In the case presented here the nature of the activity was that in calling for an investigation of psychiatry in the Soviet Union, the participants moved from issue to issue and passed the initiative from group to group. Similarly, there were others who felt that psychiatrists in the United States also have conflicts of interest as participants in the legal system. On any one of these issues, the analyst might find other groups who have competing claims or who are, or would be, allied with the groups described. There certainly are other groups interested in various other issues in the Soviet Union, and a fuller analysis of those interests would direct research toward the development of data on the activities of those groups. Thus, the data presented in this chapter might be analyzed as a case in point of social problems activity in the Soviet Union in which protests against the treatment of Jews, the censorship of art, the restriction of religious expression, and other putative conditions are compared. Such an analysis may lead to comparisons between the processes of social problems development in communist and noncommunist societies. Moving in another direction, the analysis of these data may focus on the institution of psychiatry as the target of social problems activity. This might lead to investigation of other claims against this institution, such as the control exercised by the medical profession over the certification of psychotherapists, the political activities of psychiatrists, the bureaucratization of psychiatric decisions in mental hospital admissions processes, or psychiatry as the representative of the state, as opposed to the individual.

This conception of the unit of analysis may provide a way of discussing how different social problems may be thought to be related. In the traditional approach, clusters of dysfunctional or otherwise harmful conditions are conceived to have common causal roots and, therefore, are expected to be interrelated. Thus, crime, disease, immorality, and alienation have all been related to poverty or to the state of the world economy. A line of claims-making activity can move from one issue to another. There may, indeed, be communities or alliances of groups, all making similar claims, complaints, or countercomplaints.

Our case study poses another question: what is the theoretical significance of sociological research, analysis, and interpretation of claims-making activity and the publication of those findings for the development of that activity? The data describe events that form the historical background of current and ongoing claims-making activity. Perhaps some members will continue to pursue the matter or some claim closely related to or arising out of the events described. While some of the facts assembled in the case study have already been published and are available to anyone interested, others are the result of interviews and analyses of documents that have not previously been published or revealed. Furthermore, while brief accounts of the controversy have been published or mentioned in news reports, no systematic presentation of these materials has yet been assembled. Is it possible that our presentation of the data and analysis might play a role in the future of this social problems activity, and if so, how would that affect its logical status in a theory of social problems? If sociologists are conceived to be participants in social problems activities as a consequence of their work, what questions does such participation raise about those who have assembled, written, and published studies of social problems? We shall return to this question in Chapter 7.

The Origins of Claims

The preceding case study permits us to examine an important issue to which we have alluded in preceding chapters, the origins or causes of claims-making activities. Let us review the background of this issue in our formulation. The traditional approach, following "common sense," tends to see the objective condition as the cause of the definition of the problem. This view is implicit in the statement, "The situation finally got so bad that people just had to recognize it and do something about it." This implies that if the situation, i.e., the objective condition, had not finally got "so bad," it would not have been recognized or defined as a problem. A similar logic is implicit in formulations that indicate the importance of explaining the subjective awareness of a problem, but then proceed to examine the condition and the causes of the condition. Such statements are consistent only within a framework that conceives of conditions and the "magnitude," or "seriousness," imputed to them as causes of the definition of the condition as a problem. They reflect the common-sense view that when problems (objective conditions) become acute, people begin to look for solutions (subjective definitions).

We have been arguing for a different kind of analysis that directly conflicts with this conception of social problems. In the first place, the statement, "The situation finally got so bad that people just had to recognize it and do something about it," is not a statement about objective conditions on the one hand and subjective definitions on the other. The first part of the statement is, in fact, as much a subjective evaluation as the second. A statement asserting that conditions got worse presupposes a perception, definition, and evaluation of those conditions. One cannot make statements about objective conditions without making such evaluations, and it is not possible to investigate "objective conditions" without generating definitions of them since conditions remain undifferentiated until they are perceived, defined, and evaluated.

Even granting this evaluative process, the common-sense notion that problem definition comes when conditions are perceived to have become more serious is not supported by empirical evidence. Poverty as a social problem is the traditional case in point here. The resurgence of poverty as a social problem in the United States was not due to a dramatic increase in poverty, or a dramatic decline in the quality of life. Quite the contrary, the quality of life is improving by all measures produced by social researchers, but that increase is apparently not sufficient to meet the more rapidly rising expectations, indignation, and demands that poverty be reduced, if not altogether eliminated.

The problem of environmental pollution is another example that demonstrates that the seriousness of conditions is independent of their definitions as problems. The dramatic increase in concern over pollution in the late sixties could not have been a simple function of the objective level of particles in the air or water. It has political roots that are not easily related to objective environmental conditions. Some writers have suggested that the quality of the environment during the 1930's when soft coal was extensively used was worse than it is today. The perception of pollution levels depends on a technology and a decision to measure it, which in turn, indicates that some have already defined it as a problem. Definitions of a condition as a problem preexist, allowing for the definition of the condition itself and subsequent statements about how the condition caused the definition. A similar logic reverses the common idea that problems lead to solutions. A prospective solution makes possible the existence of the problem by proposing that some obnoxious aspect of life, heretofore thought to be unalterable ("nothing can be done"), might be alleviated.

In sum, empirical and theoretical considerations lead us to reject the notion that the objective conditions might somehow help us explain the subjective elements of social problems. In our own reformulation, we have found it necessary to recast these subjective elements as social problems activities since the methodological problems of operationalizing the concept of "society's defini-tion" seemed insurmountable. We have transformed the question of the ori-gins of definitions by asking: where do social problems activities—claims-making and responding activities—come from? How would we expain their origins? If neither the objective conditions nor value judgments explain them, what does?

Claims-making activities do not emerge from nowhere. Other activities lead up to, prepare, and set the stage for them. We shall emphasize the devel-opment and unfolding of claims, the contingencies of their development, and the delineation of careers in the activities organized to assert and press claims. Consequently, interest in the prehistory, or origins, of definitions of social problems is not intended to explain them by virtue of their antecedents, or to explain them away by identifying their causes. Rather we describe the context and background of social problems, their social bases. The question of how far back we must begin our analysis if we seek to construct the history of a particular social problem is both a practical and a theoretical matter.

The prehistory, or the origins, of a social problem activity does not differ in kind from the activity itself. The seamless web of events insures that our treatment of the origins of claims-making will be the same order of analysis as the study of claims themselves. The events that lead up to claims-making must be described in the same way. Since the thread of continuity is what holds the data together, we seek to identify the beginning point of a particular group's interest and participation in the preliminary and preparatory stages of claims-making.

Not all such preparations will lead to social problems. Some may be aban-doned, some groups may disband before they ever get to the stage of making a claim. The case presented in this chapter suggests that committees within professional associations may be a spawning ground for social problems. If one seeks to observe the origin of social problems activities, such committees might be good places to monitor. In many instances no social problem will develop, but in others, claims-making may emerge. Theoretically, such monitoring makes it possible to observe the beginnings of social problems.

7

The Natural History
of Social Problems

Although the value-conflict school was largely an oppositional or critical view of social problems, Fuller and Myers presented one major positive tool for the development of empirical research. They offered a natural history model and illustrated it with an empirical case in point, the rise of a trailer camp problem in Detroit between 1920 and 1937. In this chapter we shall examine their analysis and Lemert's (1951a) critical response to it. Fuller and Myers set off in a promising direction; the assumptions underlying their model of natural history are crucial to the development of an empirical sociology of social problems. However, as in their more theoretical statements, there are certain ambiguities that made the model vulnerable to Lemert's criticisms. We think that Lemert's findings may be used to revise and extend Fuller and Myers' natural history model rather than to reject it. Accordingly, we shall first discuss the original natural history formulation, then present Lemert's criticism of it, and finally propose a more general and less mechanical model of social problems.

TRAILER CAMPS IN DETROIT

Fuller and Myers began their discussion of the trailer camp problem with a conception of social problems that emphasized their emergent and dynamic qualities:

> *Social problems do not arise full-blown commanding community attention and evoking adequate policies and machinery for their solution. On the contrary, we believe that social problems exhibit a temporal course of development in which different phases or stages may be distinguished. Each stage anticipates its successor in time and each succeeding stage contains new elements which mark it off from its predecessor. A social problem thus conceived as always being in a dynamic stage of "becoming"*

*passes through the natural history stages of awareness, policy determina-
tion, and reform....The "natural history" as we use the term is
simply a conceptual tool for the examination of the data which constitute social problems. (1941b:322)*

Fuller and Myers traced the origins of the trailer camp in Detroit to
the spring of 1920. However, they found no social problems activity
until a number of years after that. Interviews with neighbors and a survey of
newspapers indicated they were "no trouble at all." By 1930 there were
four camps, and by 1935 there were nine.

*In five of these nine communities, the inhabitants made no pretense of
camping, but removed the wheels from their trailers, mounted them on
saw horses and two-by-fours, and settled down to a semi-permanent
existence. (1941b:322)*

During the decade 1925 to 1935, there were a growing number of items
in local newspapers concerning trailer camps. At first they expressed
"curiosity and amusement," but after 1930:

*The tone of the items rapidly took on a note of concern and alarm.
Complaints of neighbors were articulated on the grounds of the
unsightliness of the camps, noises, odors, immorality, crime and property depreciation in the surrounding districts....Awareness was
registered in official statements of organized civic authorities, such as
health agencies, the police, the school functionaries, almost as soon as
protests were being registered by local neighborhood groups. (322)*

Following establishment of a state of awareness, there emerged a stage
of policy determination, and interest groups began to discuss what ought to be
done. Fuller and Myers identified the following groups as participants in
this process: neighborhood and taxpayer groups, trailer manufacturers,
real estate organizations, parent-teacher associations, women's and men's
clubs, and administrators in government offices such as the police, health
officials, common council, social workers, and school boards.

Conflicts of interests over proposed solutions arose among groups who
had different and incompatible interests. Fuller and Myers portrayed the city
officials as protecting and defending "the basic organizational mores of the
community, such as private property, public health, education, and relief of
the distressed." Neighborhood and real estate groups wanted the trailers
eliminated. On the other side, the Coach Trailer Manufacturers' Association
contended that "trailer homes are the solution of the housing problems of the low-income family." It was joined by labor unions and

civil rights groups. Fuller and Myers identified the period 1935 to 1937 as the period of policy determination.

The final stage of a social problem, reform, had only begun to take place as Fuller and Myers wrote their account. The machinery of government had begun to move, starting to put policy into action. Experts moved in to solve technical and legal matters. They proposed legislation restricting trailer camps to certain locations in the city and subjecting them to licensing, inspection, and supervision. However, health and school authorities had not yet taken action, and thus the problem "seems to be on the border of transition from policy determination to reform."

LEMERT'S REPLICATION

A decade later Edwin Lemert sought to replicate the findings of Fuller and Myers in California. His article posed the question, "Is There a Natural History of Social Problems?" and his answer seemed to be *no*. Specifically, Lemert focused on the three stages of awareness, policy determination, and reform and attempted to amass California data to verify the existence of these stages.

In regard to awareness:

Following Fuller and Myers we expectantly turned to the files of the newspapers in the several California cities to study the articulate reflection of the value conflicts over trailer camps. However, we were promptly struck by the relative absence of controversial reporting and editorial discussion of such establishments. In none of the cities, as far as we were able to determine, did anything like a public interest and concern with trailer camps come to a critical focus in the newspapers. . . . In none of the communities we studied did an awareness of trailer camp problems become the generalized, multi-group, multi-sided phenomenon that was claimed for it in Detroit.

With respect to the stage of policy formation:

The authors of the concept of the natural history of a social problem held that policy formation takes place locally on three interrelated levels: First, discussion on an informal basis among neighbors; second, discussions by organized pressure groups; third, discussion among specialists and administrators. . . . The ends of civic action are largely the subject matter on the first two levels, while means become the subject at the administrative level. . . . Search as we would, we were unable to discover any but the most rudimentary indication of a process of this sort in our selection of California communities.

With respect to the stage of reform:

In searching for evidence of such a stage of reform in our investigations of trailer camps in California cities we were everywhere impressed by the limited and uneven success of efforts at reform and by the continued frustration of administrative regulations. . . . While the formal apparatus for regulation was established in all five communities, it did not follow that the apparatus worked.

Lemert concluded his discussion:

We can say with considerable certainty that the Fuller-Myers formulation of a natural history of social problems is inapplicable to the rise and regulation of trailer camps in California cities. Furthermore, it appears to be an insufficient conceptualization of the interplay of public opinion in culture conflicts in modern urban society. (1951a:218-220)

Several possible conclusions may be drawn from this exchange. Lemert thought that the concept of natural history was inadequate. In his introduction he refers to its "apparent anachronism, its threadbare ideology and meager empirical materials" and he certainly rejected the particular natural history proposed by Fuller and Myers.

Those data do suggest that trailer camps developed in different ways in Detroit than in Southern California. One important difference was that California had had a history of tent cities and auto camps that predated the appearance of trailer camps.

Several of these camps were sponsored by the city of Los Angeles in public parks; others grew up spontaneously on the ocean beaches. These early tent camps gave communities the experience to deal with the trailer camps which succeeded them. As we shall see later, this had an important effect upon the history and policy formation toward trailer camps in the communities.

A second difference was that the trailer problem was defined as one aspect of the larger problem of workers migrating to California from drought-stricken Oklahoma and Texas:

The public reaction to trailer camps was simply a minor phase of the swelling community antagonism toward undesirable migrants in general, the so-called "Okies." (1951a:219)

Many California communities that had no trailer camp controversies passed bills and ordinances regulating them. In fact, twenty-three such communities had no trailer camps at all. Lemert also pointed to county, state, and national action on the problem and suggested that Fuller and Myers erred in focusing only on the local Detroit community. While some communities relegated supervision over trailers to the health department, others failed to act decisively because they could not decide "whether trailers are vehicles or whether they are dwellings." (1951a: 222)

Finally, Lemert suggests that the very period during which Fuller and Myers turned their attention to trailer camps was:

> ... a "mad interlude," during which it was seriously feared that the house trailer was about to revolutionize the social life of the nation. Following the peak of agitation over trailers in 1937 rumor and myth subsided to the point where they could be more objectively evaluated in terms of the special problems they presented. (1951a:221)

In short, Lemert found that trailer camps were defined differently in California than they were in Detroit, and his perspective on the problem was broader. He examined the problem in more communities, showed awareness of political action at the county, state, and federal levels, and was more removed from the prejudices of the moment in gathering and analyzing his data. It is easy to agree with Lemert that Fuller and Myers were premature in projecting their interpretation of the trailer camp problem to a much broader class of problems. Their model is quite mechanical and rigid in contrast to their conception of social problems as "always being in a dynamic state of becoming." There is no doubt that the empirical materials they presented were insufficient to support an assertion that social problems progress through the stages of awareness, policy formation, and reform.

Do Lemert's valid criticisms warrant the total rejection of the natural history model for the study of social problems? We think not. Let us review the use of this sensitizing concept in sociology or related disciplines. Clifford Shaw (1931) used the concept in a work entitled *The Natural History of a Delinquent Career.* Lyford Edwards (1927) used it in *The Natural History of Revolutions.* Louis Wirth (1927) examined the natural history of ghettos. Robert Park (1955) used the concept in "The Natural History of the Newspaper" and in many of his other writings as well. In applying the concept of natural history, each sought to move from descriptions of specific cases to generalizations about the *type* of phenomenon in question. The concept also directed them to examine sequences of events, to seek the processual character of development, and to orient their analyses to the emerging and unfolding lines of social activity. We see these as major features of the natural history concept, and we believe that they can open a vigorous line of research in the sociology of social problems.

INDUCTION AND GENERALIZATION

Park's writings reveal the basic underlying concern that is expressed in the concept of natural history. This is most clearly displayed in his writings on the nature of the sociological enterprise and its relationship to other disciplines. He emphasized that sociology should examine the nature and development of institutions. For example:

> *What is needed is not so much a history as the natural history of the press —not a record of the fortunes of individual newspapers, but an account of the evolution of the newspaper as a social institution. (1955:176)*

Park was concerned not only with the differences between history and natural history, but with how changes in emphasis could transform history into sociology:

> *As soon as historians seek to take events out of their historical setting, that is to say, out of their time and space relations, in order to compare them, and classify them; as soon as historians begin to emphasize the typical and representative, rather than the unique character of events, history ceases to be history and becomes sociology. (1955:194)*

> *The sociological point of view makes its appearance in historical investigation as soon as the historian turns from the study of "periods" to the study of institutions. The history of institutions, that is to say, the family, the church, economic institutions, etc. leads inevitably to comparison, classification, the formation of class names or concepts, and eventually to the formation of law. In the process, history becomes natural history, and natural history passes over into natural science. In short, history becomes sociology. (1955:202)*

Park emphasized not only the differences, but the connections between history and natural history. History is the portrait of the individual example; natural history is the collective portrait of the type:

> *Natural history is nothing more nor less than an account of an evolutionary process—a process by which not the individual, but the type evolves. (1955:36)*

The concept of natural history, then, was much more than a hypothesis or a theory of a specific phenomenon. It contained an image of the sociological mandate itself, an insight into what makes the work of the sociologist distinct from those in closely related disciplines. It suggested that the sociologists' interest would be comparative; that they would spend more time constructing classifications and categories out of individual case histories and less time amassing and compiling these case histories from primary sources.

When sociologists used the term *natural history,* they invoked this image of their mandate even when they did not fulfill its requirements. It is evident that one cannot write a natural history of social problems from the study of a single case. Properly speaking, *a* social problem can have only a history. Social problems as a category may have a natural history, that is, a common portrait. An individual case cannot. Fuller and Myers, Shaw, Edwards, and Park tried to emphasize those aspects of the phenomena they studied that struck them as generic without developing a comparative perspective that would have allowed them to verify these hunches. Their aim to arrive at generalizations, or universal statements, empirical summaries, or collective portraits of types of phenomenon is still a valued intellectual activity even if it is rarely achieved.

The limitations of the individual case study are still a drawback of much sociological research. It is a common practice to describe the details of a single instance and then to speculate on the more general categories it may exemplify. Glaser and Strauss (1967) have commented that sociologists often create more formal theories by attempting to "write up" from one level of analysis to another by replacing the more concrete and specific terminology with a more general set without having made the comparative analysis that would permit this.

One procedure of research has attempted systematically to construct collective portraits from accounts of individual cases. This is the method of analytic induction. Given the widespread interest in generalizations, it is puzzling that this method has not received more attention and use. Since we shall devote some attention to rehabilitating the concept of natural history, it is profitable to outline an empirical procedure that might make the research on the natural history of social problems a reality.

Analytic induction proposes to construct universal empirical generalizations of a class of phenomenon, a collective portrait of elements common to every member of the category. (Znaniecki, 1934) Its method is the following: choose an example of the phenomenon under study and construct an account of this one case. Then add another case. If the account of the first case does not also cover the second case, two operations are possible: (1) modify the definition of the category to exclude one of the cases, or (2) alter the account or explanation so that it covers the additional case as well. Then choose a third case and perform the same operation. Continue the process until no further modifications of the account are necessary and no further redefinitions are required to exclude deviant cases. The result of this form of research is a true natural history, an account of those elements common to all members of a category. Robinson (1951), in a thoughtful essay, asked if such accounts are truly explanations of the activity, or if they simply are empirically grounded definitions. (See also Turner, 1953.) While such logical questions remain this research method would help fulfill the requirements of the concept of natural history. In this spirit Lemert might have used his empirical materials as a second case in point and modified Fuller and Myers' account of trailer camps so that a more general account, and not simply a rejection of their theory, would have been the product.

The analytic induction method in sociology has been used with some success in the study of drug addiction (Lindesmith, 1948), embezzlers (Cressey, 1951), and marijuana smokers (Becker, 1963). Each of these studies described patterns in the sequence of individuals' behavioral development. The construction of explanations by this method is demanding for it insists that there be no negative cases. The explanation must cover each and every case. Whether it is possible to use this method in social problems research is an open question.

EMERGENCE AND DEVELOPMENT

One use of the term natural history, then, has stressed the term natural and called attention to the generalizing goal of the sociological enterprise. The second term directs sociologists to constructions of histories, to descriptions of how things develop over time. Park stated that "the sociological point of view makes its appearance in historical investigation...." This directs the researcher to organize data over time, to have a dynamic open-ended model that reflects the conception of society as an ongoing process. The symbolic interactionists who have made the greatest use of this conception of society insist that social phenomena must be studied and analyzed as an emergent sequence of events. Natural histories, then, are based on sequences of events common to the histories of particular cases whether they are persons or institutions.

While the term natural history is still used in sociology, it is no longer the distinctive expression of this conception of social phenomena. The term *career* has in recent years come to represent this perspective in sociological theory and research. It is most widely used and developed in the study of work and occupations and also in the study of deviance. While the term career directs attention to sequences of events and lines of activity, it has acquired a double meaning that obscures the difference between history and natural history. The term is commonly used to refer both to the development of an individual's unique biography and to the general pattern associated with those in the same job or position. The first is clearly related to individual history or biography, the second requires an analysis of many biographies and is associated with *natural history* analysis. Thus, *career* comprehends both the development of individual behavior and experience and the pattern common to persons who share a social position.

The data used to construct the individual histories set the limits for natural history analysis and interpretation. The common or generic elements of the collective history must be culled or inferred from the individual cases. However, this is possible only if these individual histories have, in fact, been gathered according to a theory that specifies variables or characteristics that include these generic elements. There is, then, something of a catch in the unfolding of this research process. We may infer the generic elements of the natural histories from a sample of histories only if those elements are already present in the individual histories. If we must gather the individual histories first, how can we insure that these generic elements will be present rather than a hodgepodge of trivial, superficial, and meaningless details? One solution is to move back and forth between collecting case materials and attempting to generalize from them. This is the procedure recommended by the method of analytic induction.

A second strategy has been to attempt to sketch out the kinds of data that are thought to include the generic elements. Authors drawing on their most general ideas of sociological theory attempt to write *hypothetical natural histories*. The purpose of doing this is to initiate the process of data gathering and generalizing—to prime the pump. One may start this pump-priming with such a hypothetical natural history or with a descriptive case study. Either may initiate the process if accepted in the proper spirit. Fuller and Myers began with a detailed case history and only the most rudimentary three-stage natural history model. It is interesting and characteristic of reciprocity between case materials and generalization that the Fuller and Myers analysis prompted James Bossard, in his commentary on that paper, to describe a much more elaborate set of stages:

1. *Recognition of the problem*

2. *Discussion of its seriousness*

3. *Attempts at reform, usually intuitively arrived at, often ill-advised, promoted by the "Well, let's do* something, *folks"*

4. *Suggestions that more careful study is needed—What we need is a survey"*

5. *Here follows some change in personnel of people interested*

6. *Emphasis upon broad basic factors*

7. *Dealing with individual cases*

8. *Another change in personnel*

9. *Program inductively arrived at*

10. *Refinements of techniques of study and treatment*

11. *Refinements of concepts*

12. *Another change in personnel (Bossard, 1941:329)*

It is evident that Bossard both responded to the Fuller and Myers materials and went beyond them. His notion that different personnel enter and leave at different stages goes beyond the trailer camp example, as does his explicit notion in Stage 4 that social research may be an integral part of the data of the social problem. This list of stages might then be used to describe or generate another empirical case in point, or it might be used to return to the trailer camp example to search for the needed information.

Surprisingly, Lemert has also proposed a checklist or agenda of topics for constructing a natural history. In an appendix to his *Social Pathology,* he included a list of subjects or activities that he recommended to students or researchers to construct natural histories of deviants. While he did not develop the notion of separate stages, it is clear that he thought that the analysis of natural history was possible.

The most recent author to present a natural history model of social problems is Herbert Blumer (1971). He used an analogy to the field of collective behavior to conceptualize the process of definition through which social problems are defined. His five stages are labeled:

1. The emergence of a social problem
2. The legitimation of the problem
3. The mobilization of action
4. The formation of an official plan
5. The implementation of the official plan

Blumer's stages and his discussion echoed much of the classic value-conflict position. He argues that objective conditions do not and cannot constitute a social problem. The process of collective definition "determines the career and fate of social problems, from the initial point of their appearance to whatever may be the terminal point of their course." (1971:301)

Blumer's five-stage model is in many ways similar to Fuller and Myers' stages of awareness, policy determination, and reform. However, he introduced an important qualification to their statement that all social problems move through each stage. Blumer emphasized that movement from one stage to the next is highly problematic. Social problems may proceed so far and fail to go on to subsequent stages. He used a concept well-known to career analyses—contingency. A contingency is a branching point between two adjacent stages of a career. The notion points to the work, decisions, or changes that must happen in order for activities to advance from one stage of a career to the next. For example, in his classic treatment of the marijuana smoker, Becker (1963) discussed the contingencies of moving from being an experimenter to being a regular smoker. This change requires that a person learn the techniques of smoking, gain the ability to recognize the effects of the drug, and decide that these effects are pleasurable. Each of these contingencies is problematic. That is, they do not follow automatically and mechanically from ingesting the smoke from a marijuana cigarette. An individual may fail to proceed to a subsequent stage of the process by failing to meet any one of these contingencies.

Blumer's discussion of the five stages of the social problems career also emphasized contingencies. On the question of emergence, Blumer noted that not all harmful conditions are recognized:

Many harmful social conditions and arrangements [do] not even make a bid for attention.... If they don't emerge, they don't even begin a life. (1971:302)

Considering the process of legitimation, Blumer was even stronger in his imagery of the selective process through which some social problems break through into public awareness and others are "choked off, ignored, [or] avoided."

A social problem must acquire social endorsement if it is to be taken seriously and move forward in its career.... If a social problem does not carry the credentials of respectability necessary for entrance into these [public] arenas, it is doomed.... it flounders and languishes outside the arena of public action. (1971:303)

At the state of mobilization for action, interest groups vie to define and redefine the problem. Sentiment, strategy, and power come into play and may not only affect the career of the social problem, but how it is redefined in order to survive. Similar transformations may take place in the next stage of the formation of an official plan of action and due to:

... compromises, concessions, tradeoffs, deference to influence, response to power and judgments of what may be workable... what emerges may be a far cry from how the problem was viewed in the earlier stage of its career. (1971:303)

Blumer's final stage, implementation of the official plan, also emphasized problematic development. "To assume that an official plan and its implementation in practice are the same is to fly in the face of facts." Such plans are often "modified, twisted, and reshaped" by "accommodations, blockages, unanticipated accretions, and unintended transformations."

Blumer stressed the problematic and uneven development of social problems. He discussed schematically that each stage in the development or the career of a social problem required a particular kind of work, and that such contingencies were neither well understood nor to be taken for granted. They should, in fact, constitute the content of the study of social problems. Again and again he stressed our lack of knowledge of these contingencies and their underlying processes:

We have a vast field which beckons study and which needs to be studied if we are to understand the simple but basic matter of how social problems emerge....

We just do not have much knowledge of this process (of legitimation) since it is scarcely studied. . . .

That students of social problems should overlook this stage (mobilization for action) in the fate of social problems seems to me to be extraordinarily short-sighted. . . . (1971:302-304)

Blumer used the idea of career to articulate a particular way of looking at the social world. In keeping with his past interests, he stressed the emergent and built-up quality of social life, the uncertain, unfolding development of social action, and the play of interpretive processes in the development of collective activities.

NATURAL HISTORY OF SOCIAL PROBLEMS: A REFORMULATION

In the remainder of this chapter we shall formulate a natural history model for the study of social problems. Our formulation shares the characteristic features of the natural history proposed by others. It should be clearly stated at the outset that our natural history model is *hypothetical:* we do not assert that the generic social problems processes are the empirically derived collective portrait of a large number of individual histories. We share Blumer's view that, in most areas, the empirical groundwork for such an analysis has not been accomplished. Our discussion is an outline of what we think such histories should attend to. It attempts to prime the pump—to arm social problems researchers with a preliminary guide to amassing first cases. As such research materials appear, empirical generalizations will replace these hypothetical exploratory and speculative ventures. We expect that much of this model—perhaps all of it—will disappear under the scrutiny of empirical materials. If so, they will have been replaced by other generalizations that better describe the range of existing individual histories.

There is much work in this field, and many of the assertions below are empirically supported. Researchers in a number of disciplines have studied social problems, reform movements, and controversies in ways that shed light on the model. There is quite a bit of research on the evolution of drug laws and policy, for example. Some of this research requires secondary analysis since it was oriented primarily toward different theoretical concerns. More recently, some work has attempted to use a social definition approach similar to our own (Reasons, 1974). Work on specific aspects of social problems also exists, for example, on the juvenile court (Platt, 1969; Lemert, 1970), sexual psychopathy (Sutherland 1950a, b), and the development of total institutions (Rothman 1971). We draw on this material for examples and instructive leads. We have not attempted to exhaust the insights offered by this literature, nor have we done the kind of systematic comparative analysis that would yield an empirically derived natural history.

Our natural history incorporates some key elements of Blumer's formulation and, we believe, goes beyond it in several respects. We adopt Blumer's conception of the problematic and uncertain development of social problems from one stage to another, agreeing with him that any other conception is a misreading of the world. We also share the implicit assumption that official and governmental agencies are a prominent party in social problems activities.

We differ from the natural history formulations of Fuller and Myers and Blumer with respect to the fate of social problems after some official or governmental response has occurred. Our predecessors posited the official response or implementation of policy as the final stage of the problem. This left the resolution of social problems suspended or unexamined. Did they assume that the problem is "solved" when the government responds? Did this imply that conditions which were objects of claims-making activities had been ameliorated? Or did it imply that there were no more complaints about the condition, regardless of its objective characteristics? Neither Blumer nor Fuller and Myers described what happens after legislation has been passed, agencies established, and programs implemented. When does the social problem cease to exist?

We attempt to deal with this question. Ours is a four-stage model, with Stage 2 corresponding to the end of the Blumer and Fuller and Myers models. Stages 3 and 4 present a way of thinking about what happens to a social problem once policy has been determined and implemented. Stages 3 and 4 represent a kind of "second generation" social problem in which the solutions to previous problems (the responses to previous demands) become the basis for renewed claims and demands.

Stage 1:   Group(s) attempt to assert the existence of some condition, define it as offensive, harmful, or otherwise undesirable, publicize these assertions, stimulate controversy, and create a public or political issue over the matter.

Stage 2:   Recognition of the legitimacy of these group(s) by some official organization, agency, or institution. This may lead to an official investigation, proposals for reform, and the establishment of an agency to respond to those claims and demands.

Stage 3:   Reemergence of claims and demands by the original group(s); or by others, expressing dissatisfaction with the established procedures for dealing with the imputed conditions, the bureaucratic handling of complaints, the failure to generate a condition of trust and confidence in the procedures and the lack of sympathy for the complaints.

Stage 4:   Rejection by complainant group(s) of the agency's or institution's response, or lack of response to their claims and demands, and the development of activities to create alternative, parallel, or counter-institutions as responses to the established procedures.

Stage 1

Social problems activity commences with collective attempts to remedy a condition that some group perceives and judges offensive and undesirable. The complaining group may or may not be the victim of the imputed condition; for example, the complaint that the welfare system demoralizes its clients may be made by an organization of social workers, clergymen, or another humanitarian group not directly subject to the condition. However, groups directly affected by the condition may act in their own interests.

Initial social problems activities often consist of attempts to transform private troubles into public issues. Stage 1 is focused on the contingencies of this transformation process. Needless to say, not all such attempts are successful; a group's problem-defining activities may elicit no response—the group may lose its constituency, be ignored by the mass media, be torn by internal dissension, fail to mobilize economic resources to sustain its activity, or give up hope.

The most critical aspects of this formative stage of social problems are the ways that complaints are raised and the strategies used to press claims, gain publicity, and arouse controversy. The objective seriousness, extent of a condition, or its presumed dysfunctionality may be relatively independent of success or failure of this transformation. That is, the relationship between "objective conditions" and the development of social problems is *variable and problematic*. The correlation between types of conditions and types of claims—and the success of the latter—are empirical questions. Since social problems are raised through the claims of dissatisfied groups, we next examine the nature of these claims and the enterprise of making claims.

The Process of Making Claims.   The making of claims and complaints is an integral part of social and political life. They are everyday activities in all societies and occur at all levels of social organization. While any sort of complaint *could* become the basis of a social problem, the vast majority of such claims are disposed of. Many may simply be ignored; others may dissolve when the claim is satisfied; still others may be bargained away, cooled out, or bought off. Some claims, however, will not be turned aside so easily, leading to further actions culminating in the establishment of a social problem. Our discussion of such claims is divided into three topics: the power of claims-making groups, the nature of their claims, and the strategies and mechanisms for pressing claims.

The Power of Claims-Making Groups.   Other things being equal, groups that have a larger membership, greater constituency, more money, and greater discipline and organization will be more effective in pressing their claims than groups that lack these attributes. While the success or failure of collective action is commonly explained by referring to a group's power as measured by such attributes, we propose that for power to become a significant element in the process, it must be expressed through the claims of the participating groups and responses to those claims.

Power, conceived as the ability of a group to realize demands it makes on other groups, agencies, and institutions, may be distinguished from a group's *claims of power*. The latter may be stated explicitly—threat of strikes, boycotts, or withdrawal of political support—or implicitly conveyed—hints of plans to create embarrassing public confrontations or various forms of nuisances or harrassment. Groups may or may not be able to mobilize the power they claim, or if mobilized, it may be ineffective in producing threatened consequences. A group may be bluffing, and if its bluff is called, it may not be able to deliver. A demonstration may be ignored, forcing the group to reveal its inability to produce the threatened "mass," or a tough political boss may question the ability of ethnic leaders to deliver the bloc vote. Alternatively, a genuinely powerful group may not be willing to expend its resources on a given issue, hoping that the bluff or threat will produce the desired results.

The Nature and Variety of Claims.   Groups may experience and express dissatisfaction in a variety of ways. Vague sentiments of displeasure can contrast with their specific complaints and pointed grievances. They may have no idea who created, who is responsible for, or who caused the imputed condition, or they may have a very specific notion of who or what is to blame. These conceptions may or may not be linked to a broader ideology or theory. Groups may have no idea of how to remedy their perceived situation, or they may have very specific programs of reform and proposals for change.

All of these dimensions of the experience of dissatisfaction will influence the kind of claims that a group will make. Let us consider some hypotheses generated by these dimensions.

1.   The more vague the sense of dissatisfaction, the more diffuse and general will be the claim and the less likely will be the recognition or response to the claim.

2.   The more vague the sense of dissatisfaction, the less able is the group to affix responsibility or propose remedies for its discontent.

3.   The less able the group is to affix responsibility for dissatisfaction, the less able it is to choose a target to which to direct its complaint.

4.   The less able the group is to affix responsibility for its dissatisfaction, the less able it is to counter the charge that it is to blame for its trouble.

This sample of hypotheses suggests that the experience of dissatisfaction affects the kinds of claims a group constructs, as well as the way their claims are expressed. Often a group may be aided in developing its claim by individuals or organizations that specialize in expressing protest. A condition may be experienced in a vague and undefined way by some groups. They may even voice complaints about it, but not effectively. Then the trouble may be picked up and seen as a classic instance of exploitation, discrimination, or corruption by a political party, labor union, professional radical, or service organization. Such groups may give coherence or a rationale to the complaint; or they may offer assistance to the group in return for support on other issues.

By entering into a coalition with others, a group may gain numbers, prestige, institutional authority, or other advantages. But group members may find that these advantages are purchased at the cost of diffusion of their issue and involvement in other issues in which they have little interest. Their own troubles may be considered only a part of the larger problem by their allies, and thus be given low priority.

Large organizations may provide sophisticated ideologies that make a complaint more forceful, although a general ideology may be a disadvantage in making visible a *specific* claim. A framework that calls for a general restructuring of society or the destruction of capitalism may obscure the specific claim or give officials an excuse for ignoring the complaint.

The Mechanisms for Pressing Claims.   The fate of a claim may depend heavily on the channels through which it is pressed, the strategies used to achieve visibility of the imputed condition, and the auxiliary personnel who play a part in this process. Identifying the audience to which the complaint should be addressed is one important stage in the complaining process. If the groups complain to the wrong party, they may get no results. They may get bad advice or directions as to where they properly should go, or they may inadvertently reveal their position to an opponent, and thus undermine their position. Frequently there may be no office to complain to since the substance of the complaint is that no one is doing anything about the imputed condition, and some organization or agency should be made responsible to deal with it. In such cases, long chains of referrals and buck-passing may occur with no organization willing to accept jurisdiction over the complaint.

Similarly, the way the press and other media are handled is important to the life history of any social issue. Such elementary devices as issuing press releases or informing the media in advance of a planned event may give a claim wider coverage. Certainly knowledge and expertise in attracting and holding the attention of the mass media are important resources or skills. The support of muckraking literature or the staging of a "national event" may be crucial in transforming private troubles into public issues and controversies.

Some methods of expressing or dramatizing complaints may come to be viewed as ineffectual which, in turn, may lead to their displacement by more dramatic means of protest. Demonstrations and hunger strikes may give way to civil disobedience, insurrection, or guerilla warfare. Protest groups may face the dilemma of insuring defeat through the use of ineffective methods or risking disaster through the use of organized violence.

Documenting a Claim.   Groups pressing a claim may be asked to document their charges or to rebut evidence that contradicts their position. This process is more complicated than simply finding out "what the literature shows" or searching for someone who is knowledgeable on the subject. The following examples suggest that the process by which persons become recognizable experts in an area is also likely to create a conflict of interest that compromises the credibility of their testimony.

Harvey Molotch described this situation in his analysis of the controversy following the oil spill that occurred in Santa Barbara in January 1969. In the months following the oil spill a variety of groups formulated claims and charges and tried to find oil experts to back up their positions. Many turned to the universities, but these were not a reliable source of willing expert witnesses:

> *Complaining that his office has been unable to get assistance from petroleum experts at California universities, the Deputy Attorney General further stated: "The university experts all seem to be working on grants from the oil industry. There is an atmosphere of fear. The experts are afraid that if they assist us in our case on behalf of the people of California, they will lose their oil industry grants." (Molotch, 1970:137)*

When a panel of "experts," appointed by ex-President Nixon, recommended as a solution the resumption of oil pumping in order to *remove* all of the oil (a process estimated to take ten years and highly favorable to the oil interests), citizen groups established that these experts' geographical data had been provided by the oil companies. The panel refused to make these data public, which led to further charges that the members of the committee were themselves linked to oil interests.

In a crisis situation and surrounded by claims and counterclaims, both citizen and law enforcement groups found that the data and expertise that they needed to document their claims were withheld by groups with whom they were contending.

A second example reveals that competing sources of expertise may be used when a group finds itself in conflict with a source of authority and expertise. Associates of Ralph Nader charged that lighting standards, the minimum level of lighting (measured in foot-candles) required in schools and public buildings, are established by groups that have a vested interest in selling electricity. The lighting lobby, led by the Better Light, Better Sight Bureau and the Illuminating Engineering Society, has consistently raised the level of light required from 3 foot-candles in 1919 to between 70 and 100 foot-candles in 1972. These groups have promoted the notion that "better" light—that is, *more* light—is good for the eyes, and that poor light hurts them.

Members of the electric power industry often occupy prominent positions on the standard-setting agencies and are described as having well-entrenched vested interests. Medical researchers, a competing source of information and expertise, have disagreed. They dispute the "better light, better sight" maxim, and argue that the medical literature does not show that poor light is harmful to the eyes:

> *There is no generally acceptable evidence that poor illumination results in organic harm to the eyes, any more than indistinct sound damages the ears, or faint smells damage the nose. (Ross, 1973:53)*

The Nader group recommended that citizen groups join together to demand that lighting levels be reduced and to expose the conflicts of interest of the illuminating engineers.

As a third example of documenting claims, Joseph Gusfield (1975) showed that the way statistics are assembled may promote the documentation of certain claims, but make others difficult or impossible to document. Statistics collected on automobile accidents make it easy to document claims about careless, reckless, and drunken drivers, but very difficult to document claims about other possible aspects or causes of these accidents. Almost all statistics focus on characteristics of drivers, which facilitates the idea of those who claim that accidents are the fault of, for example, drunken drivers.

> *What is not presented is revealing of the general scheme of conceptualization with which facts are developed. . . . Such data as age of vehicle, brand and model (e.g., Dodge Polara), weight and other matters describing the vehicle design do not appear. Nothing is collected or presented which would indicate the way in which death or injury was sustained, such as the shock entailed in striking ground after emission, or the puncture resulting from collision of the body with a protruding object. . . .*
>
> *The distance between deaths and nearest emergency medical facilities, or the one-way or multiple direction of roads is not tabulated for accidents or deaths. Neither are the interstate or state highway systems distinguished. . . .*
>
> *Nothing is presented that bears on the journey to work, vacation usage, shopping, passengers, going home or other queries that place the automobile in a context of caution or risk. Neither are elements of social structure introduced that might relate income and information to automobile maintenance. (1975:294)*

The statistics collected reinforce the view that the driver is the cause of traffic accidents and deaths. The statistics that are *not* collected are the ones that might allow others to document claims that poorly constructed roadways, badly designed cars, and the lack of emergency health facilities produce higher death rates from accidents. Those wishing to pursue such social problems activities would have to begin by collecting their own documentation, but anyone wishing to complain about drunken drivers need only consult the National Safety Council's annual report.

Assertions of Claims and Social Controversy.   Social problems arise from the statements by groups that certain conditions are intolerable and must be changed. Such actions may provoke reactions from other groups that prefer existing arrangements or who would stand to lose something if they were altered. Such groups may challenge the claims of the protesting group, mount their own campaign, and lobby against proposed changes. This may result in conflicts between groups that do not use the same values or who have opposite interests in the condition in question. Such conflicts may increase the visibility of debate and facilitate the creation of public awareness of the imputed condition.

This controversy is the culmination of Stage 1. A given social problem may remain at this stage indefinitely, it may quickly be transformed into the next stage, or it may falter and die.

Stage 2

The idea that the natural history of a social problem is divided into stages suggests that the career of the phenomenon may be divided into several periods, each characterized by its own distinctive kind of activities, participants, and dilemmas. When governmental agencies or other official and influential institutions to which claims might be put respond to the complaints of some group, the social problems activity undergoes a considerable transformation. This transformation begins when the agencies start to recognize a group and respond to its complaints. The bases of this recognition may be diverse. The group may have brought considerable pressure to bear on the agency through confrontation tactics, mass media campaigns, demonstrations, or threats. It may have applied economic pressure, such as the threat of a boycott, or used political influence, or the agency may have recognized that it had something to gain by taking over and controlling the issue.

The formal recognition of the group may range from passive acknowledgment of the claim to active attempts to control, regulate, or eliminate the condition at issue in the claim. Any of these responses is likely to give the protest group a degree of recognition or standing that it did not have before. The activities of Stage 1, the attempts to call attention to a condition and define an issue, are almost entirely unofficial, conducted without the sanction or seal of social authority. With recognition of its claim, however, the group may be asked to participate in official proceedings on the problem, to meet with the mayor or testify before a congressional subcommittee hearing.

At this point it finds that it is no longer just a protest group, but the bonafide spokesman for a constituency that may be much broader than the original group. It may find that groups that previously had shunned it now expect it to press *their* claims as well. It may be called upon for more documentation of its claims than previously, and it may be asked to offer solutions as well as complaints. Even the simplest response to the claims may bring about a transformation in the protest group or create new organizational crises for it.

The response of an official agency to a protest group may be the result of a long struggle to gain standing. This may take the form of trying to convince some agency to assume jurisdiction over an issue, or it may take the form of convincing someone that the group has a real and material, rather than a merely theoretical, interest in the proceedings. In the process, the group's crusade may have become a cause célèbre, and its achievement of standing may be viewed as its finest hour. Disinterested groups or moral crusaders may have particular difficulties in gaining standing because they are not affected by the condition they protest. Such groups may be told to mind their own business, or may have to attach themselves to those who are actually affected by the condition in order to press their claim. The American Civil Liberties Union, for example, must find injured parties who are willing to go to court in order to raise constitutional issues, because the courts will not take jurisdiction over debate in principle only.

While official response may give the protest group its finest hour, it may also represent the beginning of the end òf its control over the claims it raises. The response to its complaints may take the edge off of its protest that "nothing is being done." The establishment of a committee to study the problem may cool the controversy and make the issue less visible in the mass media. Although the group may be called to testify before the committee, it often finds itself cast in the role of providing information, rather than defining and negotiating the nature of the problem. The committee may seek out other and opposing views on the topic, reducing the original group to simply one voice among many. When the hearings are over, the members of the committee will be the new experts and authorities on the subject. While the original group may comment on the report of the committee, it is that report that will define the issues, summarize the facts, and put various groups into perspective and into their places. Thus, as official and powerful agencies or institutions begin to take part in the social problems activity, they may lend prestige to the original protest group, but at the same time may begin to overshadow and thus reduce the significance of its activities. Finally, the responding agencies may take over the issue, make it their own, and neutralize or eliminate the original protest group.

Social problems that reach this stage of development may still die or disappear. The committee and its report may disenfranchize the original protesting groups, which subsequently may become demoralized and fall apart. The committee may or may not recommend that actions be taken to satisfy the claims; and these recommendations, if made, may not be enacted.

Studies of the activities and reception of commissions of inquiry in Great Britain and in the United States reveal vastly different patterns. Writing about the British Royal Commissions, Hanser said:

> *I know of no student of the Royal Commission in the 20th century who does not regard it with the highest esteem . . . it is never charged with dishonesty or violation of civil rights, with being composed of "front" men for an anonymous staff which does all the work, or with being subservient to the government. (1965:45-47)*

Further, the Royal Commissions have a reputation for producing significant (although sometimes unpopular) recommendations and for successfully getting their proposals adopted.

In contrast, presidential and congressional investigating commissions in the United States are notorious for their partisanship, their violations of civil liberties, their long-windedness, and their inability to influence governmental policy or get their recommendations adopted (see Popper, 1970 and Marcy, 1945). Commenting in 1965 on U.S. attempts to build commissions equivalent to the British system, Hanser remarked:

> *All would be in vain if the national leadership, whether from inertia, intellectual incompetence, or inability to stand up to vested interests, were consistently to ignore its recommendations. The dismal record of disregard of the rare advisory groups that have really performed well is ominous. (1965:234)*

The reaction of the American government to the commission reports on obscenity and pornography, marijuana, and violence confirm this trend in the American system. This pattern fosters the belief that commissions reform by public relations, in which the commissions to study a problem are taken to be substance of reform itself. While the commission may be set up in the heat of controversy when many protest groups are active, by the time the report is finally issued several years later, the groups may no longer be around or interested. Or they may have staked their hopes in the commission and lose their battle when the commission itself loses. Commissions may be the burial ground of a great many social problems.

In order for a social problem to continue to exist beyond this formidable hurdle, an institution must be created to deal with the claims and complaints concerning the condition in question, or some existing institution must be mandated to expand its jurisdiction to include this responsibility. When institutions are created, the social problem cannot disappear so easily.

The creation of such institutions may require legislation of a special kind and also the allocation of money, personnel, and physical facilities. Such agencies legitimate, institutionalize, and routinize the handling of complaints. Once created, they assume a life of their own. Those who staff them may develop vested interests in the operation of the agency, which then may become directed more to satisfying the *complaints* about the imputed conditions than to their amelioration or eradication. Thus, when agencies lobby for larger budgets, they emphasize that they are doing their job of dealing with complaints about the condition, but also claim that the extent of the condition is increasing and they need more money. Stage 2 is complete when complaints about some condition have become domesticated and routinized by some agency that develops a vested interest in doing something about the complaints, though not necessarily in dealing with the conditions to which the complaints refer.

Stage 3

We have suggested that when social problems activities culminate in the creation and establishment of procedures to deal with claims, those activities may diminish and even disappear. The intent of those who negotiate with the social problems group to establish such procedures may range from a genuine attempt to work out a solution to the claims to a cynical and disingenuous maneuver to mollify and defuse the social problems activities with no intention of ameliorating or rectifying the imputed condition. Regardless of intent, established procedures may be misconceived or inappropriate to the claims and demands they were designed to handle; the procedures may focus on remedies for the imputed condition, but fail to satisfy the demands of group members *as complainants*. For example, an agency may establish a program to rectify specific conditions raised by protestors, but claim that these changes "had been in the works" anyway and were not in response to protest. Agencies may do this to foster the image that all protest is ineffective, even when they are actually responding to it. In such cases protest groups may persist, even as reform is taking place, in order to force an admission from the agency to "set the record straight."

At the other extreme, the established procedures may, in fact, turn out to be a public relations solution in which the imputed conditions are ignored on the view that the social problems activities can be "cooled out" by establishing a committee, creating a liaison position for "increasing communication," and programming regular meetings to "decide issues" that are never resolved. Edelman has termed this process the "dissemination of symbolic satisfactions." He observed that "the most obvious kinds . . . are to be found in administrative dicta accompanying decisions and orders, in press releases and in annual reports. *It is not uncommon to give the rhetoric to one side and the decision to the other.*" (1967:39) (Emphasis added.)

As a consequence, assertions about the inadequacy, inefficacy, or injustice of the procedures may themselves become the conditions around which new social problems activities are organized. The groups engaged in these activities may not be the same as those involved in Stage 1 social problems; some will have disappeared after the negotiation of procedures in Stage 2. Other groups may find they lack the sophistication for dealing with the maneuvers of organizational personnel. Still others, however, may have set up "watchdog committees" to monitor the implementation of the negotiated procedures and thus stand ready to press claims in renewed social problems activities.

The important and distinctive feature of Stage 3 social problems, then, is that the claims are not concerned directly with the imputed conditions asserted in Stage 1. Rather, the claims are made against the organizations established to ameliorate, eliminate, and otherwise change those conditions. Thus, Stage 3 activities are not concerned directly with the conditions imputed in Stage 1, but with organizational procedures and methods of dealing with clients and their complaints. This may be illustrated by the difference between claims about unsanitary conditions in meat-packing plants and subsequent claims about the availability of control agents to complainants, their indifference toward the complaints that *are* registered, and corrupt practices in inspection of the conditions. Even with the best of intentions, the dynamics of bureaucratic processes may generate new sources of complaints. Agencies set up to consider all complaints equally and universalistically may later be charged with insensitivity or ritualism. Clients may claim that the agency is indifferent to the details of their particular case, and that they have become "just a number."

Stage 3, then, makes a distinction between claims about conditions that characterize social problems activities in Stage 1, and claims about the manner in which the procedures negotiated in Stage 2 function to deal with those imputed conditions. Procedures established in Stage 2 provide for the routinization of claims—complaints about pollution are directed to the environmental control agency; claims about unfair business practices might be referred to the Better Business Bureau; complaints about suspected phone taps might be taken to the phone company or police. But Stage 3 claims are generated when, for example, the environmental control agency itself is accused of licensing polluters of the environment, the Better Business Bureau is said to be in league with the local businessmen against consumers, or the assertion is made that it is the phone company or the police who are installing phone taps and monitoring them. Here, the complaints are against the very agencies that have been established to process the complaints in question. Stage 3 activities may be intensified when responsibility for handling such claims is distributed among several agencies, creating a system of passing claimants from one office to another, each denying responsibility for "that kind of problem."

The outcome of Stage 3 social problems activity may be a renegotiation of procedures, reform of existing practices, dismissal of a high-level administrator, and possibly the establishment of a new, more specialized agency. Such outcomes may effectively routinize Stage 3 claims, but possibly with explicit watchdog provisions to monitor the effectiveness of the claims-processing procedures. Alternatively, Stage 3 activities may generate an atmosphere of fundamental distrust of institutionalized procedures, an attitude of cynicism, resignation, and despair, and a lack of confidence in established institutions in general. This distrust of various institutional attempts to deal with complaints seems characteristic of many contemporary social problems activities. The gap between the creation of a regulatory agency and the sense of doubt and cynicism among social problems groups about the intention as well as effectiveness of agency efforts is becoming progressively narrow. Classic problems associated with bureaucratic procedures and charges of unresponsiveness of "establishment" agencies to the clients they presume to serve has created a militancy in social problems activities that explicitly questions the good faith of those agencies. If this lack of confidence in institutional processes is an historical trend, Stage 3 social problems may increasingly move into Stage 4 activities.

Stage 4

A new stage in the development of social problems occurs when groups base their activities on the contention that it is no longer possible to "work within the system." Their focus shifts from complaints and protests against the establishment procedures to creating and developing alternative solutions for their perceived problems. Such attempts concentrate on a local community and its problems—activities that occur in every area of social life. Residents of neighborhoods or minority groups who claim lack of police protection form vigilante patrols for their own communities. Underground newspapers emerge to provide news for and about populations ignored by the conventional press. Food co-ops develop to fill the demand for specialized products at reasonable prices. Independent political parties form to express opinions rejected by the major parties.

These activities are organized by claims that challenge the *legitimacy* of established institutions and their procedures for processing claims. The challenges may be generated by a group's experience of having been "given the runaround," of being mollified by "smooth PR types," and by outright dismissal of complainants by control agencies. They may also be more direct expressions of the generalized lack of confidence in and distrust of "solutions" that established institutions are willing to consider and implement.

Social problems in Stage 4 develop in two directions: (1) the creation of alternative institutions as a means of developing a social and political base for radically changing the existing procedures; or (2) disaffiliation and withdrawal from the institutional system to create alternative institutions as limited solutions for group members. Both of these developments are contingent on the definition of established institutions as "hopeless," the rejection or disaffiliation from the established system, and the decision to work outside the system.

These two lines of development, however, reflect a major difference in orientation. The first might be characterized as value-oriented, the second as interest-oriented social problems. The alternative institutions created by value-oriented social problems seek to establish those institutions, not only for their members, but for the society at large. The primary concern of interest-oriented activity is to create a viable solution for the members of the group, requiring only a negative relation to the established system, that is, to be allowed to pursue, without hassle or harrassment, their own solution.

The free school movement provides examples of the two types of orientation. One faction of the movement is engaged in radical criticism of the educational establishment through manifestos, articles, and books as well as by practicing new forms of educational methods with a view toward transforming the conventional system. The other faction is attempting to form free schools in rural as well as urban settings, taking as its primary task to provide alternative educational systems for its members.

The free school movement also provides an example of a frequent outcome of Stage 4 social problems, co-optation. Attempts to create alternative institutions outside of the system may produce a new set of experts in the given field. They may be the leaders of various experiments in creating and running new kinds of institutions. Experiences of this sort may be recognized by establishment organizations even though developed outside of their jurisdiction. Successful and workable alternative institutions may attract the interest of established institutions who must answer their critics. They may attempt to take over or to co-opt the alternatives developed and make attractive offers to the leaders and experts of social problems groups.

Established institutions may substantially change in this way. For example, the government may invite leaders of the free school movement to participate in conferences, compile bibliographic references, or accept grants to evaluate the alternative methods of education. These invitations may serve the established systems in a number of ways: they drain off leadership from groups that threaten institutional dominance; they co-opt old critics into its structure, enabling them to claim credit for the innovations; they insulate leaders from the members of the group, thus discrediting them and reducing their future effectiveness in organizing social problems activities.

The two types of orientation to Stage 4 activities are diametrically opposed with reference to relations with the established system. Insofar as both of them achieve their goals, they have markedly different consequences for that system. A successful value-oriented group would establish its program as *the* institutional form and, thus radically transform the existing system. In contrast, a successful interest-oriented group would remain apart, always vulnerable to the possibility of the revocation of tolerance or indifference on the part of the established system that is a condition of maintaining the alternative.

SOME FURTHER CONSIDERATIONS

Our approach basically takes a grass-roots view of social problems in which popular movements, as well as interest groups, agitate to bring social conditions to official agencies for change or amelioration. Official governmental response to such activities has been conceived as the major criterion of their effect and success so that social problems are commonly viewed as those conditions that are recognized and included as a formal part of the society's institutional agenda. This emphasis pervades the writings of the early value-conflict school, as well as of more recent writers. Blumer's treatment of social problems parallels his earlier discussions of collective behavior and social movements. Ross and Staines' (1971) attempt to focus the political science literature on the definitional process emphasized the role of government and the relevance of literature on politics and interest groups. Most recently, Armand Mauss and his colleagues (1975) defined social problems as a type of social movement characterized by champions of reforms and causes. Our own formulation also directs attention to reformers and crusaders on the one hand and to governmental response on the other.

While these two classes of actors are important participants in the process in which social problems are constructed and defined, we have attempted to guard against the conception of social problems as limited to the activities of social movement and interest groups, legislative bodies, and regulatory agencies. These groups and their activities represent just a segment of social problems; they do not exhaust the range of actors, activities, or sources of data on how social problems are defined. Furthermore, these participants do not always play the roles stereotypically assigned to them, *nor does a focus on the political activities in which they are engaged insure a consistent treatment of the definitional process of social problems.*

Attention to grass-roots movements and official response also leads to a unidirectional view of the definitional process. But governmental and other official agencies not only respond to expressions of popular concern, they may also define and foster them. For example, Becker (1965), Galliher and Walker (1977), and Dickson (1968) have described how a government agency initiated the marijuana social problem. While they disagreed on whether Harry Anslinger, Director of the Federal Narcotics Bureau, or the force of the governmental bureaucracy should be given credit for the marijuana tax act, they agreed that there was no public outcry or popular crusade against marijuana use. In fact, an agency of government set out to convince both the public and the Congress that marijuana should be regulated. The former was accomplished through articles originating in the Bureau and published in popular magazines; the latter was directed through a strong lobby for increased budgets for the Bureau and a wider mandate for drug control activities from Congress.

A similar argument has been made about the rediscovery of poverty as a social problem. Political candidates are continually searching for issues which will aid them in getting elected. This enterprise may lead to wide-ranging social problems programs. In such cases, it is not clear whether the candidate can usefully be thought of as a social crusader or reformer or as a part of the government. John F. Kennedy's discovery of poverty in the West Virginia presidential primary in 1960 is a case in point. Here the stereotypic roles of initiator and responder become vague and less useful as descriptive or analytic devices.

A third example should caution us against the mechanical assumption that the people initiate and the government responds. Some have suggested that a government may sometimes attempt to create one problem in order to divert attention from another problem. For example, some environmental groups have suggested that in the late 1960's a conspiracy of high governmental officials sought to funnel discontent and protest away from the Vietnam war by creating or encouraging the antipollution movements and environmental movement. The theory was that such movements would tend to find their villains in private industry, not in government. This would allow the Democratic administration to move against big business and claim credit for attacking its traditional foe. Most of all, they hoped it would deflect protest from the war in Vietnam.

Whether or not we believe that the environmental movement was begun or intensified in this way, it is clear that any theory of social problems should not automatically rule out such possibilities. The grass-roots model, like the conspiracy model, should be viewed as an empirical hypotheses, not as an ideological choice. Labeling an argument as a conspiracy theory does not make it wrong. Similarly, a grass-roots model is not necessarily more correct just because we live in a "democratic country." Furthermore, the discovery that one social problem was created through either of these models does not prove that all others were created in the same way. If we show that the antiwar movement was a grass-roots effort, that tells us nothing about the sources of the environmental movement.

Much of the present literature on regulatory agencies does not offer the materials pertinent to an analysis of the social problems definitional process. Such studies may document the history of agencies, describe how they work, or whether they effectively control the powerful interests they are empowered to regulate. They usually do not describe how an agency's activities are called into question, the kinds of complaints that are registered, how they are registered, and by whom and with what effect. Nor do they indicate how such complaints are managed by the agency, or how serious complaints are differentiated from those of cranks or fringe groups. These are not questions that generally guide students of governmental agencies; indeed, the issues that we might consider problematic and interesting are frequently taken for granted as routine features of the agencies' organized activities. The researcher who makes an assessment of agency functions against some specified standard often does not describe, for example, the politics of setting those standards.

Similarly, there is a large literature on social reformers, crusaders, and social movements that has obvious relevance for the study of social problems. We emphasize the importance of reformers and action organizations as initiators of social problems activities. The literature on such actors and activities has its own concerns that diverge from a social definitional perspective. Biographies of social reformers often attempt to glorify their historical role or claim importance for the work of a figure heretofore ignored or unappreciated. Sometimes, a movement may be thoroughly discredited in existing histories. For example, Gusfield (1966) pointed out that there were no histories of prohibition that regard it as anything but a foolish, misguided effort. Our perspective would lead us to suspend an assessment of the senselessness or reasonableness of the assertions and contentions of any group, focusing instead on how members came to make and press them in claims-making activities.

IS THERE A NATURAL HISTORY OF SOCIAL PROBLEMS?

In part, this question is not yet answerable, and, in part, the question is miscast and inappropriate. The concept of natural history, as it developed in the 1930's and the 1940's, was a way of speaking about the emerging enterprise called academic sociology. Its practitioners, including Fuller and Myers, never fully attempted to live up to the rigorous strictures that were later imputed to it. Some sociologists have attempted to develop research procedures that would make it possible to discover natural histories if, in fact, they exist. They have enjoyed some limited success, but have not been widely adopted or followed. The successful application of a closely related concept, career, however, suggests that the attempt to identify common sequences of events or stages of development in a category of phenomenon should not be dismissed summarily.

To date, all natural histories have been either hypothetical constructions or somewhat overextended case studies. Neither provide convincing testimony to the possibility of successfully discovering a sequence of stages common to all social problems. None of the practitioners of analytic induction claims that the use of the procedure itself guarantees success. It is possible that in any attempt no amount of mental ingenuity will produce such elegant empirical generalizations as those of Lindesmith, Cressey, and Becker. Many activities have no natural histories, but only histories.

The search for common or typical stages of development is not always rewarded. Indeed, recent developments in the study of industrialization are turning away from two decades of attempts to identify the stages through which a country goes when it industrializes. Attempts to determine that recently industrializing countries duplicate the stages of countries that underwent the process earlier have failed. In this area, the concept of natural history is in low repute and has been widely abandoned. Newer approaches have sought, instead, a larger framework—a world system approach—largely as a way of understanding why countries that industrialize later differ from those that industrialized earlier. Thus, the very differences becomes the phenomenon to be explained, and the search for common elements or stages is simply abandoned.

Wallerstein's comments on the concept of stages of development clearly delineate the logical character of the problem:

> Not only does the misidentification of the entities to be compared lead us to false concepts, but it creates a non-problem. Can stages be skipped? This question is only logically meaningful if we have "stages" that "co-exist" within a single empirical framework. If within a capitalist world-economy, we define one state as feudal, a second as capitalist, and a third as socialist, then and only then can we pose the question: Can a country "skip" from the feudal stage to the socialist stage of national development without "passing through capitalism"? But if there is no such thing as "National development" (if by that we mean a natural history) and if the proper entity of comparison is the world-system, then the problem of stage-skipping is nonsense. If a stage can be skipped, it isn't a stage. (1974:390)

It may well be the case that a similar approach to social problems will also fail. It may be extremely difficult to define and redefine the category in a convincing way. If this occurs, all is not lost. The original counsel of the natural history concept to examine sequences of events and to document unfolding lines of activities will have produced a rich literature on how definition of social problems are constructed. If these varied and heterogeneous statements resist universal generalizations, they should nonetheless lead to a more gradual theoretical development. Detailed analyses of individual cases should shed light on how future cases should be analyzed. In a barely begun substantive area without an established research tradition, a hypothetical natural history may serve as a temporary procedural manual, a checklist of things to attend to, and a first order of business.

8

Teaching Social Problems

In this final chapter we will describe a classrom strategy for organizing a course in social problems that uses a social definition perspective. By focusing on the activities through which definitions are constructed, we believe a vigorous and empirically oriented program of research and teaching is possible. Whenever a group or an individual engages in claims-making activities, the student of social problems will find something of interest. This approach greatly enlarges the resources for teaching social problems. Again, we are guided by the study of occupations which has capitalized on the fact that students can easily observe and encounter phenomena relevant to class discussions. This is not so easily done in social problems courses as they are traditionally organized and taught. The causes of various conditions or their presumed dysfunctionality are difficult, if not impossible, to observe directly, if indeed they exist at all.

When organizing our undergraduate course in social problems, we designed a number of projects, or assignments, derived from the social definition perspective. These projects are intended (1) to bring the students into contact with the "raw materials" of social problems phenomena;(2) to introduce some fundamental tools of observation and research; and (3) to show how the students' own attitudes and actions exemplify the processes discussed in class. The class in which these projects were initially developed met two hours a day, five days a week for six weeks—a total of sixty hours, which is roughly the equivalent of a two-quarter course in a normal school year.

The students in that class completed one project per week during the six-week summer session. There were no exams—the projects constituted the sole bases for evaluation. No textbook was used. Instead, required readings were drawn from the critical literature referred to in preceding chapters, and later in the course, a wide variety of descriptive materials related to each project was used. (Each project described below is followed by a list of recommended supplementary reading.) Approximately twenty-five students were enrolled in the class, but we believe the same format would be viable with up to forty students, and if graduate teaching assistants are available to supervise conferences, the projects could be used in classes enrolling the large numbers of students typical of most social problems courses.

Six projects are described below in the order that we presented them to the students. Projects 1 and 2 utilize the students' own cultural values and knowledge as a resource with which to locate social problems. They are designed to indicate the relevance of the theoretical perspective to events and feelings that students have already experienced. Projects 3, 4, and 5 address large-scale social problems and introduce the students to important bibliographical tools and research skills. They require intensive work in the library and may require the instructor to learn certain skills along with the students. Librarians are usually delighted when instructors send their students to explore reference and bibliographical resources available in their collections. Unfortunately, far too many students and faculty members are ignorant of their use, but librarians are often willing to come into the classroom or to conduct tours and seminars in the library on the most effective use of reference materials. Projects 3, 4, and 5 should be discussed with reference and government-documents librarians so that they can more effectively help students with these assignments.

Project 6 sends the students out into the community to use interview and participant-observation techniques to encounter social problems activities in a natural setting. Such projects are more time-consuming, require closer supervision, and are better suited to small classes. In addition, the feasibility of field projects depends on the nature of the surrounding community; the opportunities in a small town are vastly different from those in a metropolitan area. However, it is possible to design field projects that are well structured *and* limited in scope.

Within the ethical limits of gratuitously stirring up trouble, field-experiment techniques may be used in which actual complaints, requests for information, or other contacts are made with control agencies, the press, or social problems protest groups. (See Gordon et al., 1973, and Divorski et al., 1973 for examples using the Freedom of Information Act.)

PROJECT 1: RECOGNIZING AND DEFINING SOCIAL PROBLEMS

The first project introduces social problems as a technical term and as a members' or common-sense category. The students' cultural apparatus—their own values and conceptions of the world—are the basic resources of the exercise. We asked them to identify five social problems in current newspaper stories. After locating social problems in this way, the student was to make explicit the criteria of membership into this category.

Some of the students identified as social problems news articles that reported the level or degree of a social condition. One example was a very short article that reported the number of traffic fatalities on a holiday weekend. In order to make this qualify as a social problem, the student had to add, "This is a problem because I feel that such deaths are a tragic waste of life." The criterion was the student's own values which helped to select or recognize offensive and objectionable conditions.

Other students used the social definition approach and classified as social problems newspaper reports of groups expressing disapproval or outrage, or making claims, complaints, demonstrations, or protests. This included groups protesting against low auto-safety standards or lax enforcement of speed limits that "result in the carnage on the highways." Their criterion focused on activities through which definitions of problems emerge and are sustained. Others noted that newspapers may take part in, as well as report on, claims-making activities. They classified as social problems editorials that called for reforms, investigative reports, and crusading columnists.

The role of value judgments also emerged in the conditions which students thought were destructive to society. The high rate of divorce and no-fault divorce were discussed extensively in the news the week this project was assigned. Some students thought the rate of marriage failure was a social problem because it weakened the nuclear family and thus threatened the American way of life. Others thought that the rate of marriage failure was the result, not the cause, of weakness in basic institutions. Such discussions demonstrated how functionalist theories are as much popular conceptions as they are scientific, value-free theories. We linked the students' diagnoses of social conditions to criticisms of functional theory and asked how these could be distinguished from their own preference and judgment of some life-styles over others.

Not only did this introductory project illustrate the role of value judgments in evaluating social conditions, it also posed the difficult problem of constructing a technical definition of social problems for the classification of the variety of materials submited by the students. We suggest as supplementary reading for Project 1: Morris, 1973, Cressey, 1967, and Molotch and Lester, 1974.

PROJECT 2: SOCIAL PROBLEMS ACTIVITIES

Social problems exist only through the enterprise of groups or individuals who create them. We asked students to consider the preparatory stages of this activity. We asked them to choose some aspect of their lives or some conditions in their community that they considered disturbing and offensive and to begin to think what they would do to get it defined as a social problem. We asked them to:

1. Describe the condition.
2. Specify why it is annoying, disturbing, harmful, unethical, destructive, or unwholesome.
3. Identify what causes the condition.

4. Describe what should be done about it.

5. Explain how one would begin to accomplish this.

Describing the condition led to activities not usually associated with sociology courses. For example, a commuting student who considered the potholes in the highway that he used to be a problem because of the danger they posed when drivers swerved to avoid them found himself walking along the road with a ruler to measure their depth. Others, who thought pollution was a problem, found they could not document their condition as directly. They relied on published reports in the daily newspaper. Still another, who thought planned obsolescence was a social problem, could not document the condition at all except to infer a conspiracy within the automotive and appliance industries to produce new models of shoddy quality, requiring expensive and dishonest repair service and parts that are scarce as well as incompatible with older models.

This project seemed to work best when focused on small-scale situations that the students encountered directly, such as conditions within their own communities. The distinction between a small-scale and large-scale condition should not be equated with trivial, as opposed to important, problems. Many conditions may become public or political issues, both within a local jurisdiction, where a small-scale condition becomes the object of attention, and at a national level, where the condition may have a larger-scale analogue or where the issue may be the proliferation and distribution of many small-scale conditions. If students wish to investigate such conditions as racism, sexism, corruption in government, or planned obsolescence, they stand a better chance of documenting the condition on a small scale within communities they know than with reference to American society as a whole. Since the investigation of such conditions would entail empirical specification of intentions, motives, strategies, and conspiracies, as well as actions related to them, the condition will always be more difficult to document than potholes, uncollected garbage, or short-weight practices. Those who chose conditions they had personally experienced were better able to document and carry through the analysis than those who chose very large-scale problems. For the latter, documentation consisted largely of assertions that the conditions existed or of vague ideological statements. These are part of the definition of the condition as a problem rather than a documentation of the condition itself.

It was sometimes unclear just what the condition in question was. One project began as a complaint about bike thefts. It subsequently turned into a grievance about how insurance companies handle claims. In the end, it focused on who had keys to the storage areas in the basements of apartment buildings. Such difficulties reflect not poor work from the student, but a basic characteristic of the natural history of social problems: the basis of the problem, the condition that constitutes the problem itself, shifts and changes over time in just such ways.

In considering what made the condition offensive, students grappled with other basic ingredients of social problems—moral indignation, value judgments, and conflicts of values and interests. The specific way a condition may give offense is variable and problematic. What is it about prostitution that offends people? What makes it a social problem—being accosted on the street, the spread of disease, the exploitation of women, spoiling a neighborhood and reducing real estate values, driving shoppers from a commercial district, deviant sexual practices, or the criminals that supposedly hang around prostitutes? The vocabulary of values that may be invoked against a condition is large and not mechanically determined by the condition itself.

Part of the members' enterprise of defining social problems is figuring out what causes the condition in question. Such analyses are part of their thinking about what should be done, who should be approached to do it, and what kinds of solutions might be effective. The students' projects revealed that sometimes these analyses took the form of searching for the person or events creating the condition. Sometimes they attempted to locate the person or official in charge of the condition and affix responsibility or blame or determine who benefited from the condition and thus would have a vested interest in it.

In searching for solutions to the problems some students suggested actions leading toward defining the condition as a social problem, but others suggested adjustments that would remove the experience of the condition without so defining it. One person, offended by the use of IQ tests in the public schools, said she would find a job in a school that didn't use such tests. There were other examples of individual adjustments that relieved the personal experience of the condition without in any way defining it an actionable or problematic object of policy or reform.

Other students did consider a variety of protest, complaining and pressure group tactics to define the condition they had chosen as a problem. Some said they would "form a group" or "find other people who felt the same way I do." Knowing how to do this was more difficult. A few said they would find some existing group that was already doing something about the condition or one that might be interested in it. For example, a person offended by potholes need not form a group of pothole haters; perhaps the automobile club would take an interest in their claim. This suggested the staggering number of voluntary associations, clubs, and interest groups that conduct just such social problems activities. Ross (1973) and Molotch (1970) offer good supplementary readings for Project 2.

PROJECT 3: SOCIAL REFORMERS
AND CRUSADERS

There is an immense literature on social reform movements and crusaders that should be much more assimilated by the sociology of social problems than it is. Most textbooks dispose of the historical background of a current problem in a few introductory paragraphs. Consequently, this literature is not made accessible to the student. Our approach to social problems implies a strong historical dimension. A discussion of how a condition comes to be defined as a problem leads naturally to a consideration of the individuals and groups that championed movements to create or change public policy toward the condition. Much of the recent empirical social problems research has an historical emphasis (see Reasons, 1974; Roby, 1969; Platt, 1969; Holmes, 1972).

Each student was assigned a specific nineteenth-century American reformer. They were to search each of the following reference tools for information about their person:

The Dictionary of American Biography

The National Cyclopaedia of American Biography

Biography Index

The Encyclopedia of the Social Sciences

The National Union Catalogue of Pre-1956 Imprints

They were to identify their person and the reform movements and social problems they were associated with. In addition to this short biographical sketch, they assembled a list of citations by and about their reformer, a list they could follow up if they were going to write a term paper. (They were not to write such a paper, however, due to time limitations and the demands of the other projects.) In addition, they kept a journal describing their encounters with reference and bibliographic resources. They described each source, its purpose, organization, and limitations. For example, the National Union Catalogue lists published and unpublished works written *by* the reformers; it has no subject index, and may not be easily used to find works *about* the reformer. The 1934 publication date of the Dictionary of American Biography is one of its drawbacks. Certain gaps or lacunae also appeared and were discussed in class, such as what one should do about the period between the publication of the D.A.B. and the beginning of the Biography Index.

As all researchers know, this reference and bibliographic work is in part a clerical exercise—searching through indexes, checking cross-listings, copying citations, keeping track of and eliminating duplication, cultivating attention to neatness, orderliness, and a compulsion for accuracy and completeness. In order to minimize the purely clerical aspects of this work we avoided very well-known reformers, those who have been so extensively treated that a student could fill an entire volume with citations. By including only lesser-known figures we designed the list to emphasize the search for citations, not the massive copying of page after page of references. Indeed, for some reformers on the list, the end product is only a handful of articles.

Few libraries contain all of the works generated through this search; libraries at new or small schools may have few or none of them. This does not affect the viability of the project since it focuses only on the use of reference and bibliographic tools. The students are not writing term papers on figures they research and thus need not consult all of the citations. They only need access to the relevant reference tools.

The reformers included in our list for the assignment were:

Lyman Beecher	Edward Jarvis
Eduard Seguin	Arthur Tappen
Carroll D. Wright	Benjamin Rush
Neal Dow	Richard Dugdale
Isaac Ray	Louis Dwight
Sarah and Angelina Grimke	Enoch C. Wines
Theodore Frelinghuysen	William Lloyd Garrison
Harvey Wilber	Frederick H. Wines
Samuel Gridley Howe	Henry H. Goddard
Pliny Earle	Horace Mann
Clifford Beers	Dorothea L. Dix
Hamilton Wright	

There is no reason why the list need be limited to names of Americar or to the nineteenth century. For more contemporary figures or for other coun tries, the list of reference and bibliographic tools would be different. The fol lowing are suggested for supplementary readings: Gusfield, 1966; Griffin, 1960; and Rothman, 1971.

PROJECT 4: A LEGISLATIVE HISTORY

One important type of social problems activity is the creation of new laws. Laws that make some act or condition legal or illegal, change the penalties of an existing crime, create social control agencies or welfare bureaucracies, modify licensing arrangements, or affirm fundamental civil rights or privileges may affect the definitions and activities of social problems. Legislation is one phase of the natural history of social problems. We asked each student to choose an issue they believed had been the subject of social problems activities and locate an attempt to use the legislative process to shape this definition. They were then to follow the progress of the bill, noting which groups sponsored, supported, and opposed the bill, what legitimating values were used, what evidence was presented, and how the issue was resolved. The bill need not have passed into law. Those that die in committee are no less interesting or revealing than those that are debated and passed. Students frequently had to choose among a variety of related bills in different sessions of Congress.

Topics such as gun control, pollution, consumer protection, women's rights, preservation of the wilderness, and drug regulations were chosen and worked well.

Like Project 3, this one required students to use a part of the library unfamiliar to most of them. It introduced them to the use of government documents as well as to social problems phenomena. They had to learn how to use subject indexes to government publications to locate bill numbers, hearings, reports, and debates. Such documents can be informative and voluminous. Sometimes the documentation was so massive that no one could have read it all in the week allotted to this project. In other cases no hearings appeared to have been held in committee and very little debate occurred as they moved to the floor for action. As public events, hearings, and debates have a certain prearranged or staged quality. Sometimes we wondered why some of the interest groups that might have been expected to follow a given issue closely did not testify, or why certain questions were *not* asked in debates on the bills.

The technical character of much legislation also raised interesting questions for the social definition approach. Frequently debates did not address issues of moral indignation at all, but seemed only to focus on technical details. What is one to make of hearings over whether the danger level of a pollutant is ten parts per million or one-hundred parts per million? Such hearings allow us to observe who has authority to speak as an expert witness and to observe the power the professions and specialists wield in shaping public policy.

In other bills it was difficult to see the relevant social problem without inside information. One student, an army officer, described opposition to lowering the educational requirements for army recruits. A variety of veterans' groups described the undesirable consequences of such a policy for the army. It was apparently widely known in the military that these groups feared that the army would become a predominantly black organization, yet not one word to this effect emerged in the hearings. This again suggested the limitation of such official data and raised the question, how can we know what legislative maneuvering and strategy are "really" about? The following references provide good supplementary readings for Project 4: Holmes, 1972; Cook, 1969; Dickson, 1968; Becker, 1963; Roby, 1969; and Sutherland, 1950a, 1950b.

PROJECT 5: SUBJECT INDEXES AS DATA

Researchers conventionally use indexes, such as the *Readers' Guide to Periodical Literature,* to locate material published on a topic. In this project, we focused on the list of subject headings used to classify and divide up the population of citations. These subject headings and the cross-references linking them are themselves historical data indicating what categories were in use during the time period of each volume. These categories change over time—new headings appear and old ones disappear. A subheading may become a main entry, indicating its increasing importance, and entries may subdivide into many finer distinctions. Cross-references (i.e., *see also* instructions) may change, indicating which items are seen as related to each other. In short, the system of subject entries constantly in revision, provides the student of social problems with data on how definitions and categories change over time.

We asked students to choose a social problem and study how its place in a subject index changed over a ten-year period. We urged them to explore a wide variety of indexes, popular as well as specialized or technical literature, newspaper indexes, and guides to legal or medical literature. One example should indicate the potential of this way of studying social problems. *Readers' Guide to Periodical Literature* has contained the entry "pollution" for over sixty years. The entry first appeared as "Pollution: See Air pollution, Water pollution."

Typically, there were very few entries under pollution itself, and under air and water pollution, there were only the occasional further cross-references such as "See Smog." In 1964, however, the pollution entry began expanding to include more items, subdivisions, and cross references. By 1971 the pollution entry looked like this:

Pollution: (33 entries)
> *See also*
> Air P.
> Pesticides and the environment
> Radioactive fallout
> Soil P.
> Space P.
> Water P.

Caricature and Cartoon: (2 entries)

Control: (48 entries)
> *See also*
> Aerospace industries—Pollution control activities
> Electronics in pollution control
> Environmental movements
> Industry and the environmental movement
> New York City—Environmental protection administration
> United States—Environmental protection agency

Economic Aspects: (13 entries)
> *See also*
> United States—environmental financing authority (proposed)
> Water Pollution Control—Economic aspects

Economic Aspects: (9 entries)

International Control: *See* Pollution Control

Laws and Legislation: (18 entries)
　　See also
　　Water P.—Laws and Legislation

Measurement: (2 entries)
　　See also
　　Air P.—measurement
　　Oil P. of rivers, harbors, etc.—management

Moral and Religious Aspects: (1 entry)

Physiological effects: (2 entries)
　　See also
　　environmental health

Protests, demonstrations against
　　See Environmental movements—marches, rallies, etc.

Taxation: (1 entry)

Colorado: (1 entry)

Europe: (1 entry)

Japan: (1 entry)

Netherlands: (1 entry)

Russia: (4 entries)

Pollution control industries
　　See also General Signal Corporation

Securities: (3 entries)

P. Control teach-in
　　See environmental movements—teach-in

P. of lakes
　　See Water P.

P. of streams
　　See Water P.

P. policy
　　See environment policy

P. Probe (organization)
　　See Environment movement—Canada

This exercise provided another approach to the study of social problems definition. It included a temporal dimension that permitted us to ask, for example, when did pollution become defined as a social problem? It also presented that definitional process from the perspective of those who monitor popular and technical publications and create the categories that we use to do research and locate information. The following reference makes good supplementary reading for Project 5: Berman, 1971.

PROJECT 6: THE EXPERTS

The expert, or expert witness, is frequently encountered in social problems activities. In theory, the expert is impartial and neutral, the spokesman neither of an interest group nor of a value position. Some people are thus disqualified and prevented from assuming the expert role; not all those who ask to testify before a hearing or commission are permitted to do so. For those accorded this role, the fiction is adopted that if they are not free of interests or emotional involvement, their professional integrity will safeguard the independence of their judgment or testimony. Where such fictions cannot be sustained, adversary procedures may be used to ferret out bias, whether conscious or unconscious, intended or inadvertent. Or, when all knowledgeable parties have compromising interests, political expediency and public relations may gloss over these embarrassing and discrediting "details" in order to "get on with it." We suggest that who finally becomes the expert on a subject is more complicated than simply "who knows a lot about this?" Under what circumstances would a policeman be allowed to speak as an expert about police brutality? A drug addict about addiction? An oil company petroleum engineer about off-shore pollution? An electric company spokesman about minimum permissible lighting levels in schools?

To begin an exploration of these questions, we asked students to choose a social problem and imagine how they might begin some program of claims-making about it. How would they begin to locate experts to testify for them, to document and legitimate their complaint? Who would be ready and willing to assume this role? Who might they ask who would decline to testify? This phase of the project required the students to invent a reasonable and realistic political strategy and examine their own ideas of where experts might be located. This frequently led to interest and lobbying groups, but students were alerted to the possibility that their experts might be exposed and disqualified as biased or partisan if too closely associated with a group having a known position. Some students uncovered "expert lists" put out by the public relations offices of several universities in the area. These are directed primarily at the news media in the hope of keeping the name of the university and its faculty before the public. Not infrequently, sociologists are listed as experts, some of whom were surprised to learn of their repute, and others who became a bit defensive when asked for their qualifications or credentials.

We also investigated who was called by the newspapers and electronic media for authoritative statements or comments on a news item. We asked students to compile a list of authorities cited on a specific social problem during a two-month period in a local newspaper. (We used the *Chicago Tribune* because it is subject indexed in the *Newspaper Index.*) After compiling a list of authorities, the students called up the reporters (such stories usually carry by-lines) and asked them why they contacted those authorities and not others.

This facet of the assignment was complemented by an account in the local journalism review (Aronson, 1974) of how the media had created an expert on a rare disease. A reporter, pressed for an authoritative comment on Reye's syndrome, had called her brother-in-law, a physician, who looked it up in a textbook for her. Subsequent editions and rewrites of the story listed the physician as a noted authority on the subject. Soon he was receiving calls from all over the country. Finally, when the two "real" experts on Reye's syndrome had apparently made conflicting statements, a national television network called him to determine "who was right." This admittedly extreme example made more visible the demands and pressures for authoritative statements that create and define expertise and package it for public consumption.

This project pushed the logic of the social definition approach to its conclusion and led to a counter-intuitive approach to the question of expertise. It was frequently difficult to separate and focus on the question, "How are experts created and credentialed?" from the quite different question, "Who knows a lot about a given subject?" Is the person cited or asked to testify *really* more expert than those not asked? Is a person who is very knowledgeable on a subject, but strongly associated with a value or political position, less an expert than one less knowledgeable, but apparently more neutral? Who would decide who is more knowledgeable? What if all of those who are knowledgeable have conflicts of interests? Does that mean there are *no* experts? The following are suggested as supplementary readings for Project 6: Rosenfield, 1949; Bernstein, 1955, pp. 113-125; Aronson, 1974; Molotch, 1970.

DIFFICULTIES OF THE PERSPECTIVE

The social definition perspective contains some counter-intuitive notions that violate common-sense assumptions. These may lead to stimulating classroom debate, but many also create some confusion. One such issue concerns the possibility of studying the causes of the objective conditions. We argued that when groups attempt to define some conditions as a problem they frequently include a causal analysis in their program of claims-making. Such analyses are *part of the data* for the study of social problems. Students sometimes interpreted this as a denial of causal analysis altogether, or thought we were saying that no one should conduct such research. However, the assertions that causes are socially negotiated understandings, or that statements about causation may be used politically, say nothing about the reality of existence of causation per se.

Similarly, we questioned the position that when problems become acute, solutions are sought and created. It makes just as much sense to argue that solutions lead to problems; a comparison with Lemert's statement (1967) that "social control leads to deviance" is instructive. The idea that something might be done to change or improve a condition previously thought incurable, unalterable, or part of human nature or fate—in short, a solution—may lead to the definition of a social problem where there previously was none. Such ideas may arise from ambitious and entrepreneurial individuals or professions seeking to create needs to serve or administer to with these solutions.

We have described an attempt to organize a social problems course around an emerging theoretical position that runs counter to the traditional approach to the subject matter. We believe that these projects are miniature and prototypical versions of the kind of research that would make the social definition approach into a full-fledged substantive field in sociology. For this reason, we have found these projects much more interesting reading than the more typical exercises, term papers, or examinations normally inflicted on both students and instructors.

REFERENCES

American Psychiatric Association
1952   *Diagnostic and Statistical Manual of Mental Disorders.* Washington,
        D.C.: American Psychiatric Association.

1968   *Diagnostic and Statistical Manual of Mental Disorders.* 2d ed. Washing-
        ton, D.C.: American Psychiatric Association.

Aronson, Neil
1974   "The Press Syndrome: Expertitis," *Chicago Journalism Review,* 7 (April)
        4-5.

Barnett, H. G.
1954   "Comment on Acculturation: An Exploratory Formulation," *American
        Anthropologist, 56* December 1000-1002.

Bazelon, David L.
1969   "The Interface between Russian Psychiatry and the Law," *The First
        U.S. Mission on Mental Health to the USSR.* Washington, D.C.:
        Public Health Service, Publication No. 1893, pp. 73-99.

1974   "Psychiatry and the Adversary Process," *Scientific American, 230*
        (June) 18-23.

Becker, Howard S.
1962   "The Nature of a Profession," in *Education for the Professions.* Chicago:
        National Society for the Study of Education, pp. 27-46.

1963   *Outsiders: Studies in the Sociology of Deviance.* New York: Free Press.

1966   "Introduction," in Becker (ed.), *Social Problems: A Modern Approach,*
        New York: John Wiley, pp. 1-31.

Bend, Emil, and Martin Vogelfinder
1964   "A New Look at Mills' Critique," in Rosenberg, Gerver, and Houghton
        (eds.), *Mass Society in Crisis.* New York: Macmillan, pp. 111-122.

Bentley, Arthur F.
1908   *The Process of Government: A Study of Social Pressures.* Bloomington,
        Ind.: Principia Press.

Berman, Sanford
1971   *Prejudices and Antipathies; A Tract on the L. C. Subject Heads Concerning People.* Metuchin, N.J.: Scarecrow Press.

Bernstein, Marver
1955   *Regulating Business by Independent Commission.* Princeton: Princeton University Press.

Birenbaum, Arnold, and Edward Sagarin
1972   *Social Problems: Private Troubles and Public Issues.* New York: Charles Scribner and Sons.

Blum, Alan F., and Peter McHugh
1971   "The Social Ascription of Motives," *American Sociological Review,* 36 (February) 98-109.

Blumer, Herbert
1971   "Social Problems as Collective Behavior," *Social Problems, 18* (Winter) 298-306.

Bordua, David
1967   "Recent Trends: Deviant Behavior and Social Control," *Annals of the American Academy of Political and Social Science,* 369 (January) 149-163.

Bossard, James H. S.
1941   "Comment," *American Sociological Review,* 6 (June) 320-329.

Bott, Elizabeth
1968   *Family and Social Networks:* 2d ed. London: Tavistock Publications.

Bucher, Rue, and Anselm Strauss
1961   "Professions in Process," *American Journal of Sociology,* 66 (January) 325-334.

Case, Clarence
1924   "What Is a Social Problem?" *Journal of Applied Sociology,* 8 (May-June) 268-273.

Cohen, Albert K., and James F. Short, Jr.
1971   "Crime and Juvenile Delinquency," in Merton and Nisbet (eds.), *Contemporary Social Problems.* New York: Harcourt Brace Jovanovich, pp. 89-147.

Cook, Shirley
1969   "Canadian Narcotics Legislation, 1908-1923: A Conflict Interpretation," *Canadian Revue of Sociology and Anthropology,* 6 (February) 36-47.

Cressey, Donald R.
1953   *Other People's Money: A Study in the Social Psychology of Embezzlement.* Glencoe, Ill.: The Free Press.

1967   "Methodological Problems in the Study of Organized Crime as a Social Problem," *Annals of the American Academy of Political and Social Science,* 374, (November) 101-122.

Cressey, Paul G.
1932   *The Taxi Dance Hall: A sociological Study in Commercialized Recreation and City Life.* Chicago: University of Chicago Press.

Cuber, John, and R. A. Harper
1948   *Problems of American Society.* New York: H. Holt.

Deutscher, Irwin
1973   *What We Say/What We Do: Sentiments and Acts.* Glencoe, Ill.: Scott, Foresman.

Dickson, Donald
1968   "Bureaucracy and Morality: An Organizational Perspective on a Moral Crusade," *Social Problems,* 16 (Fall) 143-157.

Divorski, S., Andrew Gordon, and Jack Heinz
1973   "Public Access to Government Information: A Field Experiment," *Northwestern University Law Review,* 68 (May) 240-279.

Edelman, Murray
1967   *The Symbolic Use of Politics.* Urbana: University of Illinois Press.

Edwards, Lyford P.
1927   *The Natural History of Revolution.* Chicago: University of Chicago Press.

Faris, Robert E.
1967   *Chicago Sociology:* 1920-1932. San Francisco: Chandler Press.

Foskett, A. C.
1971   "Misogynists All: A Study in Critical Classification," *Library Resources and Technical Services,* 15 (Spring) 117-121.

Frank, L. K.
1925   "Social Problems," *American Journal of Sociology,* 30 (January) 462-473.

Freidson, Eliot
1970   *The Profession of Medicine.* New York: Dodd, Mead.

1971   *Professional Dominance.* New York: Atherton.

Frosio, Eugene T.
1971   "Comments on the Thomas Yen-Ran Yeh Proposal," *Library Resources and Technical Services,* 15 (Spring) 128-131.

Fuller, Richard
1937   "Sociological Theory and Social Problems," *Social Forces,* 15 (May) 496-502.

1938   "The Problem of Teaching Social Problems," *American Journal of Sociology,* 44 (November) 415-435.

1939   "Social Problems," in Robert E. Park (ed), *An Outline of the Principles of Sociology.* New York: Barnes and Noble, pp. 3-59.

1942   "Morals and the Criminal Law," *Journal of Criminal Law and Criminology,* 32 (March) 624-630.

Fuller, Richard, and Richard Myers
     1941a   "Some Aspects of a Theory of Social Problems," *American Sociological Review,* 6 (February) 24-32.

     1941b   "The Natural History of a Social Problem," *American Sociological Review,* 6 (June) 320-328.

Galliher, John F., and Allynn Walker
     1977   "The Puzzle of the Social Origins of the Marijuana Tax Act of 1937," *Social Problems,* 24 (February) 367-376.

Gibbs, Jack
     1966   "Conceptions of Deviant Behavior: The Old and the New," *Pacific Sociological Review,* 9 (Spring) 9-14.

Glaser, Barney G., and Anselm L. Strauss
     1967   *The Discovery of Grounded Theory: Strategies for Qualitative Research.* Chicago: Aldine.

Goode, William J.
     1960   "Encroachment, Charlatanism, and the Emerging Professions: Psychology, Sociology, and Medicine," *American Sociological Review,* 25 (December) 902-914.

Gordon, Andrew, Jack Heinz, Margot Gordon, and S. Divorski
     1973   "Public Information and Public Access: A Sociological Interpretation," *Northwestern University Law Review,* 68 (May) 281-308.

Gouldner, Alvin
     1970   *The Coming Crisis in Western Sociology.* New York: Avon Books.

Griffin, Clifford S.
     1960   *Their Brothers' Keepers: Moral Stewardship in the United States, 1800-1835.* New Brunswick, N.J.: Rutgers University Press.

Gusfield, Joseph R.
     1966   *Symbolic Crusade: Status Politics and the American Temperance Movement.* Urbana: University of Illinois Press.

     1975   "Categories of Ownership and Responsibility in Social Issues: Alcohol Abuse and Automobile Use," *Journal of Drug Issues,* 5 (Fall) 285-303.

Hanser, Charles J.
     1965   *Guide to Decision: The Royal Commission.* Totowa, N.J.: Bedminster Press.

Hewitt, John P., and Peter M. Hall
     1973   "Social Problems, Problematic Situations, and Quasi-Theories," *American Sociological Review,* 38 (June) 367-375.

Holmes, Kay Ann
    1972   "Reflections by Gaslight: Prostitution in Another Age," *Issues in Criminology,* 7 (Winter) 83-101.

Homans, George
    1967   *The Idea of a Social Science.* New York: Harcourt Brace Jovanovich.

Horowitz, Irving L., and Martin Liebowitz
    1968   "Social Deviance and Political Marginality," *Social Problems,* 15 (Winter) 280-296.

Horton, P. B., and G. R. Leslie
    1965   *Sociology of Social Problems,* 3d ed. New York: Appleton-Century-Crofts.

Hughes, Everett C.
    1971   *The Sociological Eye.* Chicago: Aldine.

Kozol, Johnathon
    1972   *Free Schools.* Boston: Houghton Mifflin.

Kuhn, Thomas S.
    1970   *The Structure of Scientific Revolutions,* 2d ed. Chicago: University of Chicago Press.

Lemert, Edwin
    1951a   "Is There a Natural History of Social Problems?" *American Sociological Review* 16 (April) 217-233.

    1951b   *Social Pathology.* New York: McGraw-Hill.

    1967   *Human Deviance, Social Problems and Social Control.* Englewood Cliffs, N.J.: Prentice-Hall.

    1968   "Social Problems," in *International Encyclopedia of the Social Sciences.* New York: Crowell, Collier and Macmillan, V. 14, 452-458.

    1970   *Social Action and Legal Change: Revolution within the Juvenile Court.* Chicago: Aldine.

Library of Congress
    1950   *Library of Congress Classification. Class H: Social Science,* 3d ed. Washington, D.C.

    1966   *Subject Headings Used in the Dictionary Catalogue of the Library of Congress,* 7th ed. Washington, D.C.

    1968   *Supplement to the Subject Headings for January to December 1967.* Washington, D.C.

    1970   *Supplement to the Subject Headings for January to December 1969.* Washington, D.C.

    1974   *Library of Congress Classification Schedules. Class H: Social Science.* Detroit: Gale Research Co.

Liebow, Elliot
    1967   *Tally's Corner: A Study of Negro Streetcorner Men.* Boston: Little, Brown.

Lindesmith, Alfred R.
    1947   *Opiate Addiction.* Bloomington, Ind. Principia Press.
    1965   *The Addict and the Law.* Bloomington: Indiana University Press.

Manis, Jerome
    1974a   "The Concept of Social Problems: Vox Populi and Sociological Analysis," *Social Problems,* 21 (Winter) 305-315.
    1974b   "Assessing the Seriousness of Social Problems," *Social Problems,* 22 (October) 1-16.

Marcy, Carl
    1945   *Presidential Commissions.* Morningside Heights, N.Y.: King's Crown Press.

Martindale, Don
    1957   "Social Disorganization: The Conflict of Normative and Empirical Approaches," in H. Becker and A. Boskoff (eds), *Modern Sociological Theory.* New York: Holt, Rinehart, and Winston, pp. 340-368.

Matza, David
    1969   *Becoming Deviant.* Englewood Cliffs, N.J.: Prentice-Hall.

Mauss, Armand L.
    1975   *Social Problems as Social Movements.* Philadelphia: J. P. Lippencott.

Medvedev, Zhores, and Ray Medvedev
    1971   *A Question of Madness.* New York: Alfred Knopf.

Merton, Robert K.
    1971   "Epilogue: Social Problems and Sociological Theory," in Merton and Nisbet (eds.), *Contemporary Social Problems.* New York: Harcourt Brace Jovanovich, pp. 793-846.

Merton, Robert K., and Robert Nisbet (eds.)
    1971   *Contemporary Social Problems.* New York: Harcourt Brace Jovanovich.

Miller, Judy
    1973   "A.P.A. Psychiatrists Reluctant to Analyze Themselves," *Science,* 181 (20 July) 246-248.

Mills, C. Wright
    1940   "Situated Actions and Vocabularies of Motives," *American Sociological Review,* 6 (December) 904-913.
    1942   "The Professional Ideology of Social Pathologists," *American Journal of Sociology,* 49 (September) 165-180.
    1959   *The Sociological Imagination.* New York: Oxford University Press.

Molotch, Harvey
    1970   "Oil in Santa Barbara and Power in America," *Sociological Inquiry,* 40 (Winter) 131-144.

Molotch, Harvey, and Marilyn Lester
    1974   "News as Purposive Behavior," *American Sociological Review,* 39 (February) 101-112.

Morris, Monica B.
    1973   "The Public Definition of a Social Movement: Women's Liberation," *Sociology and Social Research,* 57 (July) 526-543.

Nisbet, Robert
    1971   "Introduction: The Study of Social Problems," in Merton and Nisbet (eds.) *Contemporary Social Problems.* New York: Harcourt Brace Jovanovich, pp. 1-28.

Park, Robert Ezra
    1955   *Society: The Collected Papers of Robert Ezra Park, Vol. III.* Glencoe, Ill.: The Free Press.

Parsons, Talcott, Robert F. Bales, and Edward A. Shils
    1953   *Working Papers in the Theory of Action.* New York: Free Press.

Platt, Anthony
    1969   *The Child Savers: The Invention of Delinquency.* Chicago: University of Chicago Press.

Popper, Frank
    1970   *The Presidents' Commissions.* New York: Twentieth Century Fund.

Raab, Earl, and Gertrude J. Selznick
    1959   *Major Social Problems.* Evanston, Ill.: Row, Peterson.

Rains, Prudence
    1975   "Imputations of Deviance: A Retrospective Essay on the Labeling Perspective," *Social Problems,* 23 (October) 1-11.

Ranulf, Svend
    1938   *Moral Indignation and Middle Class Psychology.* Copenhagen: Levin and Nunksgaard.

Reasons, Charles
    1974   "The Politics of Drugs: An Inquiry in the Sociology of Social Problems," *The Sociological Quarterly,* 15 (Summer) 381-404.

Robinson, William S.
    1951   "The Logical Structure of Analytic Induction," *American Sociological Review,* 16 (December) 812-818.

Roby, Pamela
    1969   "Politics and the Criminal Law: Revision of the New York State Penal Law on Prostitution," *Social Problems,* 17 (Summer) 83-110.

Rogers, A. C.
1910a   "Report of Committee on Classification of the Feebleminded," *Journal of Psycho-Asthenics,* 15, 2 (December) 61-67.

1910b   "Editorial: The New Classification (Tentative) of the Feebleminded," *Journal of Psycho-Asthenics,* 15, 2 (December) 68-71.

Rokeach, Milton
1968   *Beliefs, Attitudes and Values: A Theory of Organization and Change.* San Francisco: Jossey-Bass.

Rosenfeld, Harry N.
1949   "Experts Are Never Right," *Antioch Review,* 9 (March) 3-15.

Ross, Donald K.
1973   *A Public Citizen's Action Manual.* New York: Grossman Publishing.

Ross, Robert, and Graham L. Staines
1971   "The Politics of Analyzing Social Problems," *Social Problems* 20 (Summer) 18-40.

Rothman, David J.
1971   *The Discovery of the Asylum: Social Order and Disorder in the New Republic.* Boston: Little, Brown.

Rubington, Earl, and Martin S. Weinberg
1971   *The Study of Social Problems: Five Perspectives.* New York: Oxford University Press.

Scheler, Max
1961   *Resentment,* ed. Lewis Coser and tr. William Holdheim. Glencoe, Ill. The Free Press.

Scott, Marvin B., and Stanford M. Lyman
1968   "Accounts," *American Sociological Review,* 33 (February) 46-62.

Shaw, Clifford R.
1931   *The Natural History of a Delinquent Career.* Philadelphia: Albert Saifer.

Skolnick, Jerome, and Elliot Currie (eds.)
1970   *Crisis in American Institutions.* Boston: Little, Brown.

Spitzer, Robert
1973   "A Symposium: Should Homosexuality Be in the APA Nomenclature?" *American Journal of Psychiatry,* 130 (November) 1207-1216.

Sutherland, Edwin
1950a   "The Diffusion of Sexual-Psychopath Laws," *American Journal of Sociology,* 56 (September) 142-148.

1950b   "The Sexual Psychopath Laws," *Journal of Criminal Law and Criminology,* 40 (January) 543-554.

Tallman, Irving, and Reece McGee
1971   "Definition of a Social Problem," in Smigel (ed.), *Handbook of the Study of Social Problems.* Chicago: Rand McNally, pp. 19-59.

Tannenbaum, Frank
1938   *Crime and the Community.* New York: McGraw-Hill.

Truman, David B.
1951   *The Governmental Process.* New York: Alfred Knopf.

Turner, Ralph H.
1953   "The Quest for Universals in Sociological Research," *American Sociological Review,* 18 (December) 604-611.

Van Dine, Alan
1972   "Under Philosophers," *Saturday Review,* March 18, 55-67.

Waller, Willard
1936   "Social Problems and the Mores," *American Sociological Review,* 1 (December) 922-934.

Wallerstein, Immanuel
1974   "The Rise and Future Demise of the World Capitalist System: Concepts for Comparative Analysis," *Comparative Studies in Society and History,* 16 (September) 387-415.

Westhues, Kenneth
1973   "Social Problems as Systematic Costs," *Social Problems,* 20 (Spring) 419-431.

Wolf, Stephen
1972   Untitled press release. American Library Association Convention, June, Chicago.

Wirth, Louis
1927   "The Ghetto," *American Journal of Sociology,* 23 (July) 57-71.

1940   "Ideological Aspects of Social Disorganization," *American Sociological Review,* 5 (August) 472-482.

Yen-Ran Yeh, Thomas
1971   "The Treatment of the American Indian in the Library of Congress E-F Schedule," *Library Resources and Technical Services,* 15 (Spring) 122-128.

Znaniecki, Florian
1934   *The Method of Sociology.* New York: Farrar and Rinehart.

Name Index

Subject Index